It's one thing to desire t̶̶̶ earth…and another to have the strategy of the Holy Spirit to do it. I believe Johnny Enlow has been a conduit of divine insight and wisdom in these pages that will accelerate our mandate to usher in revival and transformation throughout the earth. I highly recommend this book.

—Dr. Che Ahn
Senior Pastor, Harvest Rock Church
President, Harvest International Ministry

This insightful book by Johnny Enlow is a fascinating unveiling of the prophetic revelation given separately to Bill Bright and Lauren Cunningham almost a generation ago. It is so relevant for us today! I commend this book for everyone desiring to be an impact player for Christ.

—Larry Tomczak
Director, International Center for Evangelism,
Church Planting, and Prayer (ICECAP)

Thank God for Johnny Enlow's new prophetic book. Enlow powerfully depicts how the Lord's Prayer will be manifested and how His kingdom will come on Earth, as it is in heaven! The message of this book—that Christians are called to more than just sub-culture, that calling and vocation are not limited to narrow religious confinement—is vital to the potency of the church. I highly recommend this world-changing book and encourage every reader to grab hold of this vision.

—Bob Weiner
Weiner Ministries International

For several decades now we have been losing the culture to secularists and liberal agendas. If we are going to reclaim the seven mountains of culture for Christ, the church must make a major shift in how we do this. Johnny Enlow has given us a master strategy to fulfill Christ's mandate to reclaim all that has been lost. Christ already paid the price, but we must now take the land. This book is a must for every serious Christ-follower who believes we are called to be the head, not the tail, by modeling Christ on Earth. It is spiritually rich with an understanding of the times and how we are to play a strategic role in the last days. Well done, Pastor Johnny!"

—OS HILLMAN
AUTHOR OF *TGIF TODAY GOD IS FIRST* AND *THE 9 TO 5 WINDOW*
PRESIDENT, MARKETPLACE LEADERS AND INTERNATIONAL
COALITION OF WORKPLACE MINISTRIES

If you have a desire to see your city transformed, you should read this book. Johnny Enlow does an excellent job of laying out God's divine strategy of how Christians can influence their communities. Not only are there seven mountains in cities that need to be reclaimed, but you will begin to realize how entire nations can be taken for the kingdom of God. This is the hour for the body of Christ to move into the harvest field and take cities. This book is on the cutting edge of God's plan for city transformation.

—CAL PIERCE
DIRECTOR, HEALING ROOMS MINISTRIES INTERNATIONAL

The strongest word that the Spirit is currently speaking to the churches relates to God's desire for His people to take dominion over every area of our society. The best template for designing the strategies to accomplish this is known as the seven mountains or the seven molders of culture. No one to date has better revealed to the body of Christ the natural and the spiritual challenges for fulfilling God's plan in each of the mountains than Johnny Enlow. I believe that every kingdom-minded leader, whether in the church or in the workplace, needs to make this amazing book required reading!

—C. PETER WAGNER
PRESIDING APOSTLE, INTERNATIONAL COALITION OF APOSTLES

If you are radical enough not just to pray for transformation and revolution in society but to live it, this prophetic blueprint can show you the destiny only you can fulfill.

—LOU ENGLE
CO-FOUNDER, THE CALL

Anyone interested in breaking through barriers to cultural transformation will want to read this book. Like a modern-day Lewis and Clark, Pastor Johnny Enlow has done an enormous service to us all in surveying the ground before us.

—LANCE WALLNAU

The Seven Mountain Prophecy by Johnny Enlow on the coming Elijah Revolution may be the most spiritually discerning book that I have read about our current times. This book truly reflects what I am seeing God doing in the global marketplace. Read it and be alert!

—KENT HUMPHREYS
PRESIDENT, FCCI/CHRIST@WORK

Finally the contemporary church is recognizing that we must be the salt of the earth in every area of society. Jesus called us to disciple nations, and Johnny Enlow does a masterful job of outlining how we as Christ's servants can fulfill that mission. The prophetic insights in this important book will equip you to be a world-changer.

—J. LEE GRADY
EDITOR, *CHARISMA* MAGAZINE

THE SEVEN MOUNTAIN PROPHECY

JOHNNY ENLOW

CREATION
HOUSE
A STRANG COMPANY

THE SEVEN MOUNTAIN PROPHECY by Johnny Enlow
Published by Creation House
A Strang Company
600 Rinehart Road
Lake Mary, Florida 32746
www.strangbookgroup.com

Scripture quotations are from the New King James Version of the Bible. Copyright © 1979, 1980, 1982 by Thomas Nelson, Inc., publishers. Used by permission.

Definitions are derived from *Strong's Exhaustive Concordance of the Bible*, ed. James Strong (Nashville, TN: Thomas Nelson Publishers, 1977) and Webster's Online Dictionary at www.websters-online-dictionary.org.

Scripture quotations marked KJV are from the King James Version of the Bible.

Cover design by Jerry Pomales

Library of Congress Control Number: 2007938625
International Standard Book Number: 978-1-59979-287-3

09 10 11 12 13 — 9 8 7 6 5
Printed in the United States of America

Acknowledgments

I WOULD LIKE TO give special appreciation to the Daystar members and staff for wholeheartedly embracing this new revelation and supporting me while I've learned to communicate it. Thank you to Karen Ruff and your intercessory team for birthing this through faithful prayer. Rachel Krause, you have been an expression of the favor of God in our lives and ministry. I appreciate your wisdom, faithfulness, and labor of love that is so obviously done for the Lord.

Honor is due my parents, Jack and Gladys Enlow, who modeled a faith that has instilled in me a love for the nations. I am grateful for the legacy my father left our family when he received his reward in heaven in 2005. Mom, I am so proud of your continual service to the Lord in Peru. I would also like to honor my parents-in-law, Ray and Cindy Tyler. Your love, prayer, and support in every way have given me wings.

Chris Tiegreen, your editing expertise and counsel have been invaluable to me in the process of writing this book. Thank you also to Allen Quain and the Creation House staff for making this such an easy process in releasing this project.

To my four daughters, Promise, Justice, Grace, and Glory, I thank you for surrounding me with hugs 'n kisses, laughter, and beauty. You have made my world rich beyond belief. As you travel with me to the nations, may you learn a passion for God that will cause you to follow Him with your whole heart.

Lastly and most importantly, I would like to thank my wife, Elizabeth, who has walked through every step of this with me. You have assisted in every level of this project from helping me find time to making sure that I actually say what I'm trying to say. You have been my greatest cheerleader and my ongoing best friend in this fantastic heavenly adventure that we walk together. I stay excited about the rest of our lives together in His service.

Contents

Foreword

WHEN I WAS a teenager I prayed that God would give me a husband that I would have to run to keep up with spiritually—I've been running for almost twenty years now! Keeping up with my best friend and husband, Johnny Enlow, has been more of an adventure than I ever dreamed of. Before we married, he assured me of two things he would never do—become a pastor or do the "missionary thing." And, of course, that is exactly what we have been doing for the last ten years!

Johnny's parents were missionaries for fifty years in Peru, and he saw how much work it took for seemingly so little fruit as he was raised during his teen years in the jungles of Peru. So, mission work and traveling to the nations was far from glamorous to him. This was a relief to me because I was simply terrified at the thought of leaving my own food, bed, and potty! Just a few years into our marriage the word "pastor" was considered a "dirty word" in our home. We found ourselves rudely awakened to the reality of false shepherds whose deception is rooted in Jezebel, and it was closer than we could hardly believe. In retrospect, we realize that God was preparing us for the real by allowing us to get an undeniable deep breath of the counterfeit. After pleading with God to bring justice to our city (and going through a lot of Holy Spirit-induced healing), His response was to ask us to be a part of raising up the real, His beautiful Bride. So now we both gladly spend our lives on Him and the church He gave His life for, here in Atlanta as well as in many nations we have had the privilege of traveling to. Johnny has taken teams on over sixty short-term mission trips where we have seen ordinary people like ourselves and our friends do great exploits through the power of God. (Jesus captured my heart so profoundly that even my fears couldn't keep me tied to my comfort, so I have traveled a good bit with him as well!)

If you're like me, you read books such as this one, and you think,

"How did the author get that revelation? How did it all play out in the midst of the mundane?" So, I thought, as the author's wife, I might give you a little insight into Johnny's journey to this place on the path. I've watched Johnny over the years as he's wrestled with God and learned his true identity as His son, apart from his career or ministry. I've watched him wrestle with questions concerning really big picture stuff, learning to dialogue with God about all that has grieved him in the body of Christ. And I've watched him lean into the presence of His Father, satisfied with His love even if he were never to get revelation or understanding, simply because he has found Him to be enough. His journey, our journey, has been one that has provoked us to deeper places of intimacy with God than we ever thought possible, and you know what happens when you find true intimacy—you find yourself impregnated with fruit that is eternal and more real than this earthly realm. I frequently tell Johnny, "We are in over our heads!" But, I wouldn't trade that reality for any other life. In that place we learn intimacy and end up birthing things that we cannot sustain ourselves, which presses us continually back into the Father's heart to receive His supernatural strategies and power.

I want to tell you, from the start of this book, that everything in it is an overflow of what Johnny has found in moments with His Papa. As he learned to simply be with Him, not looking for ideas for a sermon or answers to questions, he would find that when their time together was over for the day, he just knew things he didn't know before. Sometimes he describes it like this: you get in His presence and just enjoy Him and it doesn't matter whether you are hearing, seeing, or feeling anything at the moment. When you walk away you find that the Lord has slipped whatever He had for you in your back pocket while you were with Him. When you need access to it, it's right there! (OK, I must admit that it sounds so easy that at times I get frustrated because personally I am one who has a hard time getting my mind to be still. But, when I do, it sure is worth the effort.)

A little over a year ago, Cal Pierce prophesied over Johnny that God was about to show him the way the kingdom of God works and that the revelation He would give him concerning the kingdom would blow his mind. Cal also said the Lord would teach him how to save a nation in a day. It was soon after that that Johnny began to have understanding of much of what he shares in this book. A few months later, after he began writing, we were at a conference and Chuck Pierce prophesied over Johnny that he saw him having great favor in the nations and that the Lord says, "Yes, a nation can be saved in a day!"

Many of you reading this have felt so torn—you have great desire to serve the Lord, but the mundane realities of work and family are overwhelming to keep up with. If things aren't going so well with your career, you may feel tempted to figure out a way to leave it all behind and sell out to God by going into what we refer to as "full-time ministry." If your career or business is successful, then you may be tempted to believe that you don't have a ministry and maybe you let God down in some way. The prophetic revelation Johnny teaches in The Seven Mountain Prophecy truly will revolutionize your thinking. You will see the answer to the question that David asked as he saw everyone frozen in fear before Goliath, "Is there not a cause?" Your heart has cried out wondering if there is something you could give God from your life that would please Him; is there not something I was created to do of eternal weight? Just like David, you will see that your years of finding God in the midst of the mundane and killing the lions and bears that came your way, has prepared you to kill giants. Like David, you will understand that the hope for victory lies in the fact that the battle is the Lord's! Just remember something that we have learned along the way—as the Lord gives you favor to "take the head off the giant," don't confuse it with love, acceptance, and approval. Favor is not His love. Favor is for the assignment. Favor is not about you deserving it or earning it. You can have significant issues in your heart or lifestyle that God is disciplining you in and still walk in supernatural favor to impact the world. That is why it's so important to always prioritize personal intimacy with Him before ministry. What we do with and for Him must be the overflow of what we have found alone with Him. And it is in that alone place of just being with Him that

His love, acceptance, approval, AND discipline are spoken into us. Never let God's favor on you get out ahead of your intimacy with Him. To the degree that you have influence, you must have equally deep places of prioritizing His presence—whatever that looks like for you.

One last story that you just have to hear before you learn how to be an Elijah revolutionary...When Johnny finished writing this book, he went to Costa Rica where he planned to preach this fresh message for the first time in its entirety outside of our local church. The plan was to teach all of it in a conference as well as an overview on Enlace TV, which airs in over sixty nations worldwide. As background info, you have to know that he has grown very accustomed to supernatural signs taking place as he travels and preaches, many of them having something to do with the electricity and lights wherever he goes. At first, this trip to Costa Rica seemed similar to other trips in that respect. Johnny is also used to sensing quite a bit of resistance in the spirit realm as he prepares to minister, but what he felt that time was incomparable. He found himself having to pray in the Spirit under his breath whenever he wasn't speaking just to maintain focus to deliver the next message in the series. He could literally feel the confrontational power this revelation carries in the spirit. He quickly realized it was way more important than he understood at that point. Throughout the days there he noticed an increase of power outages every time he spoke about the seven mountains and everywhere he went. It became obvious that it was no coincidence. For example, when he was opening his mouth to say the first word of the message for international TV, the power blew at the station for no apparent reason. Fortunately they were able to switch to their backup source during the normal 10-second delay. So, at one of the last meetings of the conference, Johnny began to share with the people why he felt there had been frequent power outages during that week. He shared that the Lord had shown him that this revelation was so powerful, so important that it be released, that our current way of thinking needed to be rewired in order to receive it—like changing from 110 voltage to 220 voltage. He told them that he had become very aware, through this "prophetic parable" of the electricity being short-circuited, that this was powerful enough revelation that it could blow the national power grid of the entire nation. As those words came out of his mouth, at 8:10 p.m. on April 19, 2007, the national power grid of Costa Rica blew and there was no electricity in the whole nation for five hours! All of that to say this—ask the Holy Spirit to give you grace to perceive what God is releasing in this hour because He is so worthy to receive what this generation has been invited to give Him. As you read, may you more clearly see your part!

—Elizabeth Enlow

# Introduction

And I saw in the right hand of Him who sat on the throne a scroll written inside and on the back, sealed with seven seals. Then I saw a strong angel proclaiming with a loud voice, "Who is worthy to open the scroll and to loose its seals?" And no one in heaven or on the earth or under the earth was able to open the scroll, or to look at it.

So I wept much, because no one was found worthy to open and read the scroll, or to look at it. But one of the elders said to me, "Do not weep. Behold, the Lion of the tribe of Judah, the Root of David, has prevailed to open the scroll and to loose its seven seals.

And I looked, and behold, in the midst of the throne and of the four living creatures, and in the midst of the elders, stood a Lamb as though it had been slain, having seven horns and seven eyes, which are the seven Spirits of God sent out into all the earth. Then He came and took the scroll out of the right hand of Him who sat on the throne.

Now when He had taken the scroll, the four living creatures and the twenty-four elders fell down before the Lamb, each having a harp, and golden bowls full of incense, which are the prayers of the saints. And they sang a new song, saying:

"You are worthy to take the scroll,
And to open its seals;
For You were slain,
And have redeemed us to God by Your blood
Out of every tribe and tongue and people and nation,
And have made us kings and priests to our God;
And we shall reign on the earth."

Then I looked, and I heard the voice of many angels around the throne, the living creatures, and the elders; and the number of them was ten thousand times ten thousand, and thousands of thousands, saying with a loud voice:

"Worthy is the Lamb who was slain

To receive power and riches and wisdom,

And strength and honor and glory and blessing!"
—REVELATION 5:1–12

In Revelation 5, we get a glimpse into an amazing moment taking place in heaven. The Father on His throne holds in His right hand a scroll with seven seals that no one is found worthy to loose. John the apostle is overcome with sadness and tears as he contemplates this heavenly reality. An elder comes to John and tells him not to weep because Someone has just shown up who is worthy to open the scroll and to loose its seven seals.

This Someone is the Lamb who was slain for us! He is described as having "seven horns" and "seven eyes, which are the seven spirits of God." The "seven horns" represent seven foundations of power that the Lamb has because of His awesome act of redemption on the cross. It is why Jesus said after His resurrection, "All authority has been given to Me in heaven and on earth." (See Matthew 28:18.) He had now paid the price not just so souls could be rescued from hell, and not just so a few could receive healing—but He had proven that He was worthy to recover all ground that had been lost in the Garden of Eden. Jesus had regained the authority to establish the rule of God upon the seven pillars of the very cultures, or infrastructures, of every nation of the earth. Second Chronicles 16:9 tells us that "the eyes of the LORD run to and fro throughout the whole earth, to show Himself strong on behalf of those whose heart is loyal to Him." The Lamb's "seven eyes" are literally looking for those whom He can send supernatural help from heaven to as they advance the kingdom of God on earth. The "seven spirits of God" represent the heavenly help and angels assigned to enforce the authority that Jesus was given over heaven and earth. That is why He followed His "All authority is mine" declaration with the great commission to "make disciples of all the nations." (See Matthew 28:19.) The

Great Commission has always been about much more than what most of us have imagined.

Back in Revelation 5:6, we see that an explosion of joy filled the heavens as Jesus took the scroll with the seven seals. The four living creatures and the twenty-four elders burst forth with a new song. Verse 10 tells the key line of the song, "[You] have made us kings and priests to our God; and we shall reign on earth." The dominion that Adam and Eve had lost was now regained and heaven was rejoicing. Millions of angels then joined in singing (v. 12)…

> "Worthy is the Lamb who was slain to receive power and riches
> and wisdom, and strength and honor and glory and blessing."

These seven attributes of majesty that He is worthy to receive each coincide with the seven main pillars of every nation's culture or society. When we speak of discipling the nations, we are speaking of these seven pillars of society that the Lamb is worthy to receive! After researching the original Greek meanings of these words, it became evident to me that power speaks of Government; riches speaks of Economy; wisdom speaks of Education; strength speaks of Family; honor speaks of Religion; glory speaks of Celebration (Arts and Entertainment); and blessing speaks of Media. The Lamb was slain, making the ultimate sacrifice, to enable us to disciple, or instruct, the nations in these seven foundations of culture so that we would in turn deliver them to Him, thus fulfilling Revelation 11:15: "The kingdoms of this world have become the kingdoms of our Lord and His Christ, and He shall reign forever and ever!" Our God is worthy that all areas of society in every people group come under His righteous rule.

In the chapters of this book I will refer to these foundations of culture, or sectors of society, as "mountains." Revelation 17 describes a "harlot" who sits on a "beast with seven heads" that are "seven mountains." This demonic entity, described as a woman, must be displaced from the mountains, or seats of power. This is our mission that we were co-missioned by Jesus to do. Jesus is the Head and we are His body. He already did His part at regaining all power and authority through the cross and His resurrection. He left earth so that He could send us the same Holy Spirit that was powerful enough to raise Him from the dead, in order that we would be able to fulfill His mandate to "go, therefore and disciple all nations." This is our unfinished business, our Promised Land that is yet to be taken. All that we need has already been provided for and there will be an accompanying favor as we accept this mission.

In the coming chapters I will highlight the seven specific areas of influence that the Lord has assigned us as the church, and then offer insight into the nature of the spiritual battles involved in this sevenfold mission. These seven culture-shaping areas—Media, Government, Education, Economy, Family, Religion, and Celebration (Arts and Entertainment)—are the key to advancing the kingdom of God in the nations.

The favor to "invade" these seven mountains is already upon us as part of God's end-time strategy to establish Him as Ruler of the Nations. I have personally begun to experience this favor, being suddenly thrust into opportunities to speak prophetically into the lives of key leaders in several nations I often visit. I have been privileged to reach presidents, congressmen, politicians, generals, captains, governors, mayors, top executives, and media personalities. This God-initiated phenomenon is taking place for many around the world and will only increase as Christians accept the mission Jesus called us to. There is a sudden surge of favor available to us to be positioned in places of unprecedented societal influence.

Today, nations with no history of Christian political leadership are coming under the influence of Christian presidents, congressmen, and other key governmental leaders. Christian educators are being drawn to the forefront and becoming known for new concepts and new curriculum for schools. Movies and art are suddenly experiencing Christian influence as never before. Christian athletes, coaches, artists, musicians, economists, lawmakers, journalists, entrepreneurs, and the like are being spiritually promoted like never before. As the world becomes darker, the true light of Christ is beginning to shine brighter. In unprecedented fashion, the church is getting an opportunity to manifest Christ's solutions for society—in an "outside the four walls" context. The Lord is raising His people up and giving them an opportunity to fulfill the entire Great Commission—to disciple nations and not just individuals.

Some are recognizing the strategic sovereignty of God in promoting them to heights heretofore unseen. Many, however, do not fully grasp the opportunity God is giving us. That is the central purpose of this book: to help Christians understand that this favor is divinely strategic and constitutes the place of each person's ministry assignment. Every believer needs to understand his or her work is not a "secular" calling, but rather a God-assigned mission!

I will also be identifying the nature of the spiritual battle that will unfold as we gain and then maintain godly influence in these society-shaping arenas. Recognizing the God-initiated phenomenon of societal favor must be followed with an understanding of the spiritual armor we must wear in order to overcome the demonic enemies that operate on the seven mountains of influence. Each mountain is under a demonic assignment specific to that particular arena. Godly influence can only be gained by operating in the opposite spirit from that which rules in the world. For example, a Jezebel spirit will try to prevent a Christian from influencing the Mountain of Celebration (Arts and Entertainment), so a believer seeking to have an impact on that mountain must maintain personal freedom from that influence. A spirit of Mammon will work to keep Christians from progressing on the Mountain of Economy (Business and Wealth). Therefore a Christian who is called to great influence on this mountain must be stripped of Mammon's influence in his own life before he can exercise any spiritual authority there. In order to succeed in bringing God's influence to bear, we must first understand the assignment and then understand the operating nature of the demonic forces that would seek to circumvent us.

I believe this book can be a helpful resource for Christian high school and college students to assist them in pursuing a biblically mandated career opportunity. Imagine beginning your adult life, focusing your passion for God on a specific area of study, knowing that you are called to transform it through supernatural, Holy Spirit-inspired strategies that would blow the world's mind. Imagine not caring about the salary or prestige, but caring only that God's righteousness be displayed for all to see in that area of society. It is crucial that young adults who are passionate for God be shown valid options for their futures besides going into typical ministry-related fields. My desire is to challenge those who want to radically spend their lives on God to ask Him which mountain He will give them radical favor to impact. The seven mountains or areas of influence are not the only seven in our societies, but they are the specific arenas that God is giving us favor to retake and bring under the influence of Christ. In order to become "the head and not the tail" (Deut. 28:13), we must capture the areas of influence at "the head" of our society. It is our spiritual poverty of vision and our poor eschatology that have kept us as "the tail" and out of our Promised Land.

The first several chapters of this book will specifically aim at correcting two faulty foundations in our lives—lack of vision and a misguided understanding of the end times. I will then devote a chapter to each of the seven arenas of assignment that are before us. They will not be exhaustive, but I believe they will be descriptive enough to serve as a significant launching point. As Caleb knew his specific target mountain at age eighty-five (Josh. 4:12), I believe this book will greatly serve to help you identify the "mountain" (or mountains) God is giving you favor to influence.

This book is both prophecy and strategy for the assignment that awaits us. The church will see Jesus' prayer fulfilled, "on earth as it is in heaven," and what you are about to read is an in-part template for how this is going to occur. I am aware that I over-generalize at times and even at times paint with strokes that are too broad—and so I ask for grace on that ahead of time! I believe these are the early stages of revelation for us regarding these truths and I trust more will be understood by many others as we continue to ask God for more clarity. In the meanwhile, don't discard the central premises I will lay out because of a detail of contention. This is a most amazing time to be alive and if you have "ears to hear" you might soon understand that better than ever before. May the Holy Spirit clarify your mission and mountain He created you to make an eternal impact on. Know that as you accept your "mission impossible," all things are possible with His favor!

Tsunami!

O N DECEMBER 26, 2004, our generation was rudely awakened to the reality of what a tsunami is and what it can
do. Off the western coast of Sumatra that day, an undersea
mega-earthquake jolted seismic sensors worldwide. It may
have been the second greatest earthquake ever to shake the planet.*

The shaking reportedly did not stop for more than five hundred
seconds—the longest quake ever in its category. It created an oceanic
trench several kilometers wide, dragging millions of tons of rock as
much as seven miles across the seabed. The entire planet vibrated at
least a half an inch, and shock waves were registered as far away as
Oklahoma. The earth's rotation was altered, and the length of its days
was shortened by a couple of microseconds. This was truly an earthquake of biblical proportions.

As cataclysmic as this earthquake may have been, the ensuing waves
that it caused did more to capture our attention. The shift created by
the quake unleashed a series of tsunamis that killed an estimated two
hundred thirty thousand people and inflicted billions and billions of
dollars' worth of horrific damage. Waves up to one hundred feet high
pounded the shores, even causing some islands to disappear entirely.
Tsunamis continued relentlessly for hours, reaching as far as South
Africa—five thousand miles away.

Never has a disaster of this magnitude been seen by so many.
Thanks to modern technology, our generation got to witness the
tragedy firsthand. Ever since that day, those who live near coastlands
do not dare to linger around when they feel the earth shake beneath
them. Every earthquake represents a potentially disastrous tsunami.
Living by shore has become a hazardous occupation.

---

* The official U.S. Geological Survey measurement is 9.1, though there remains
some question as to whether the quake might have actually been 9.3.

WHAT IS A TSUNAMI?

A tsunami is a displacement of water that produces a new, suddenly higher sea level. Its name comes from two Japanese words: *tsu,* meaning "harbor," and *nami* meaning "wave." This was the name given to it by Japanese fishermen who, upon arriving back at the harbor after a day at sea, were shocked to find it destroyed. Out in the deep, they noticed nothing; a tsunami is barely perceptible in deep waters. Only as it approaches shore—at a speed sometimes as much as five hundred miles per hour—does it begin to push the waters up and form a tidal wave. Unlike a normal wave, which is created by water and air currents, a tsunami is formed from an earthquake that shifts the earth's tectonic plates and displaces a massive amount of water. It can also be caused by other cataclysmic events—a meteor hitting the ocean, for example, or a large piece of land collapsing into the water. Technically, however, a tsunami is simply a sudden rise in sea level, and it's most often caused by an earthquake.

HOW DO YOU KNOW WHEN A TSUNAMI IS APPROACHING?

There is no way to know a tsunami is approaching—at least not conclusively. There are no fail-proof warning signs. Sometimes there's the evidence of water dramatically receding from the shore, but many places hit by the tsunami of '04 did not see this phenomenon. Because tsunamis are so hard to register in the high seas, it's a real challenge to accurately predict if, when, and where they will manifest. Since that devastating tsunami, warnings have often been issued in many places where a tsunami has *not* developed. Even with all of our current technology, predicting one is still about as accurate as a weather forecast—always a matter of likelihood, never of certainty. Detection of a large regional earthquake prompts only a warning that the *potential* for a tsunami exists and to be on alert if near the shore.

How Can Tsunamis Be Prevented?

Once enough energy has been released to create a major displacement of water, there's no stopping a tsunami. It's going to come ashore—somewhere.

Signs on some California beaches offer advice about how to prepare for a potential tsunami:

Tsunami Hazard Zone: In Case of Earthquake Go to Higher Ground

Every sensation of seismic movement prompts is, in effect, a test run. If neither higher ground nor an inland route is a logistical option, the only other recourse is to find the building with the strongest foundation and hardiest building material.

It's not hard to predict what will be destroyed when a tsunami hits shore:

- that which is built too close to the sea,

- that which is made from inferior building material and/
  or resting on a weak foundation, and

- those who are living in either of the above scenarios.

No house on a mountain range has ever even been splashed by a tsunami, and no person living in such a place has ever lost his or her life from a tsunami. This is a very important thing to note. A tsunami is not inherently evil. It's just a new water level that occurs *suddenly.* High ground and high-grade building material are the basic defenses to protect one from the devastating effects of a potential tsunami. Where we respect the awesome and unpredictable power of the sea, there is no damage—only adjustments to a new sea level. However, there is still no way to avert the fact that after the tsunami you will have to deal with a completely overhauled landscape below you. I am, of course, specifically pursuing the metaphorical truth and its effect.

A SPIRITUAL TSUNAMI

I'm convinced that a spiritual tsunami, this one with positive results, has already been released. I call it the Elijah Revolution. Even as the Asian tsunami of 2004 came in many waves—the third being the deadliest in many spots—so too will this next tsunami come in a series of waves. We'll delve later into all the parallels between the last tsunami and this one, but the bottom line is that the Elijah Revolution will change the landscape of society; everyone will have to make at least some kind of adjustment. Eye has not seen, nor has it entered into the heart of man, the things that are about to take place upon planet earth. The earth is the Lord's and the fullness thereof—and very soon, everyone will know it. (See 1 Corinthians 2:9 and Psalm 24:1.)

An Elijah Revolution

SOCIETY IS OBSESSED with extreme makeovers. Reality shows feature homes, faces, and even relationships being radically and quickly overhauled. These programs are announcing that the world is unhappy with the status quo; we want a quick and extreme shift away from what we've known. It's a desperate search for happiness and true love, and a great example of the "rocks" of society crying out for redemption. The world doesn't know exactly what it's looking for, but it does know to look for something different. Staring down the rifle barrels of hopeless situations—AIDS, terrorism, drugs, pandemic plagues, ethnic wars, religious wars, the breakdown of the family, famine, and hopeless political situations in the Middle East and elsewhere—people realize that a radical, earth-shaking shift is needed. The groans and labor pains of creation are manifesting (see Romans 8:22), even from Hollywood. The world is hungry for supernatural answers and ripe for sudden and profound transformation.

A tsunami is an agent of extreme makeover. It dramatically impacts the landscape. The coming Elijah Revolution will have transforming dynamics as powerful as a tsunami, and it will affect the entire world.

It will also affect the church. While something in the heart of people is drawn toward God, His followers have done such bad public relations on His behalf that it's hard for the world to see Him. The church is still attempting humanistic solutions to the problems society faces, and our attempts aren't much more successful than those of unbelievers. The older generation is dying in church, and the next generation is refusing to enter a dead church. People who are interested in experiencing presence, power, and authenticity are instead offered baby food or entertainment. The church is in as much need of a radical shift as the world's systems are.

Movies, TV, video games, and all other forms of entertainment are increasingly delving into the dark side of that which the church has neglected to manifest in the light. When the people's hunger for the supernatural isn't satisfied in the church, their only other option is to seek out false imitations of the real thing. Because most branches of Christianity haven't embraced the prophetic gifts, psychic networks are making billions of dollars—even from Christians—by delivering the counterfeit. We have been so afraid to preach and demonstrate the God of the impossible that we've opened a door for the entertainment industry to quench people's thirst for the supernatural through shows and movies featuring witches, demons, and sorcerers. We warn of the dangers of the Harry Potter series while denying the validity of true prophecy and healing for today, even though signs and wonders are scripturally non-negotiable. That's extremely hypocritical.

In 1 Corinthians 14, Paul explicitly detailed the importance of prophecy above all things except love. It is to be valued above the other gifts (verse 1), exceeding even speaking tongues, which Paul himself espoused and commanded church leaders not to forbid (verses 5 and 39). Paul's strongest statement about prophecy comes in verse 39, where he instructs us to "covet to prophesy." This word is not just permission to allow prophecy; it describes it as an objective to be earnestly pursued. The word *covet*—*zeloo* in the Greek—means "to burn with zeal." We are not simply to be open to prophecy or to passively wait for it, or even to use it as an exciting additive to our Christian walk. Rather, we are to burn with zeal for recognizing God's voice here on earth and speaking it forth.

Prophecy will be a major thrust of the Elijah Revolution. It will restore the voice of God among the affairs of men. The spiritual tsunami is coming in to perform a work of disambiguation—to clarify things that are ambiguous—as Elijah did when he called out to Israel:

> How long will you falter between two opinions? If the Lord is God, follow Him; but if Baal, then follow him.
> —1 KINGS 18:21

He then called down fire to convince Israel of who God is because

18

they really weren't sure. Likewise, this Elijah Revolution tsunami will sweep through both the world and the church, and it will leave no doubt as to who God is. The question no longer will be, Is there a God? but rather, What am I going to do about it?

THE MEANING OF REVOLUTION

A revolution is defined as:

1. a drastic and far-reaching change in ways of thinking and behaving;

2. the overthrow of one government or system and its replacement with another;

3. a sudden or momentous change in a situation.

Its antonyms include the terms *stagnation* and *status quo*. The incoming Elijah Revolution tsunami is going to eradicate stagnation and the status quo. Things will never be the same again. All three definitions of the term *revolution* will be evidenced. It will be a "sudden and momentous change in a situation," it will "overthrow" one system and replace it with another, and it will bring about a "drastic and far reaching change in ways of thinking and behaving." It will be metamorphic in the sense that it is not coming to improve or slightly upgrade our present reality. It's coming to overhaul and transform *everything* that has to do with how we think or act.

WHY AN ELIJAH REVOLUTION?

It is important for this revolution to carry with it a description and definition of just what kind of a revolution it is. The word *revolution* as a stand-alone word is not a very satisfying term. It implies a fight against the status quo without defining the nature of the replacement. Many have been motivated by revolution for its own sake, but that only joins the spirit of lawlessness that is increasing today across the earth. That would only further aggravate underlying societal ills. A movement of revolutionaries will always carry a spirit of rebellion unless it clearly articulates and presents a valid replacement system. We can't just be *against* things; we have to know what we are *for*. If not, we will find ourselves in a similar category as guerrilla movements in many nations. They know what they are against, but rarely can they articulate what they stand for.

We can already see this dynamic—a thirst for change—at work in churches in the United States. People are clearly unhappy with the status quo. They are tired of going to church as spectators of a boring, passionless ceremony. People are leaving mainline denominations and traditional churches in droves, not because they're losing interest in God, but because they are gaining interest in God. The spirit of religion is so persistent in mainline churches that it has suffocated the movement of the Holy Spirit out of church. Not only can most churches' meetings function perfectly well without the Holy Spirit, they couldn't function if He actually did show up.

That's why the doctrinal statements of many churches and denominations are carefully crafted to make sure the Spirit cannot surprise them with unexpected or unusual gifts or manifestations. He's invited to a meeting occasionally, but few really expect (or want) Him to show up. As long as His presence is unnoticeable, He's welcome.

That kind of church is already dead. It just hasn't been buried yet. But the Elijah Revolution will cause formerly "dead" churches to explode with the fires of God in them, while those that reject the Revolution will wither, die, and disappear. The tsunami will either resurrect churches or bury them.

A rapidly expanding house church movement is sweeping the United States. Some of it carries the spirit of the Elijah Revolution, and some of it just carries a spirit of rebellion and independence. Some home church gatherings are virtual anti-churches. They don't want anything to do with traditional church. In doing so, they have cast off even biblical mandates for church life. A spirit of lawlessness is attached to some expressions of this movement, and, as a result, members don't have to listen or submit to anyone, they don't have to commit to anything, and they can even keep all their money—except for offering a tip here and there.

As we delve more into the nature of the Elijah Revolution, we'll need to check ourselves to see what our true motivation is. Are we just against something? Or are we also clearly for something? It is very important that we not just be opposed to the dead church system, but that we also extract "the precious from the worthless" and allow ourselves to be built into something definable. God is not against pastoral leadership. He is only against pastoral leadership that does not equip the saints for the work of the ministry. He is against pastors who are "hirelings" but not those who love "the sheep" (John 10:11–14). Though He opposes pastors who manipulate for offerings, true principles of giving and first fruits are still very valid. The Elijah Revolution will sweep through the church and recover that which is good while washing away that which is polluted.

WHO WAS ELIJAH?

In order to fully embrace the Elijah Revolution, we need to understand who Elijah was, what he did, and how his life applies to us today.

Elijah first shows up in 1 Kings 17 as the prophet God called to confront Israel with her Baal worship. His archenemy was Jezebel, a prophetess of Baal who tried to kill him time and time again. Elijah was able to decimate the prophets of Baal and to finally anoint Jehu, the one who would destroy Jezebel. As his closing act, he released the "double portion" mantle to Elisha before being taken up into heaven by a whirlwind.

We want to look at the prophecies of a coming "Elijah" and what his focus will be. The most significant prophecy comes from Malachi 4, after which the Bible remains silent for four hundred years. The last two verses of the Old Testament leave us with an expectation of an Elijah Revolution that will precede the Lord's return:

> Behold, I will send you Elijah the prophet, before the coming
> of the great and dreadful day of the Lord. And He will turn the

hearts of the fathers to the children, and the hearts of the children to their fathers lest I strike the earth with a curse.

—MALACHI 4:5–6

This passage establishes that a revolution will take place *before* the Lord returns. I believe it will be a revolution of mercy because its purpose would be to avert catastrophic judgment.

The key to restoration is for the hearts of fathers and their children to be turned toward each other. This turning is profoundly needed at every level of church life and every level of society. The lack of true fathers has created devastating voids. It's a major contributing cause of loose sexual morals and homosexuality, as well as of many illnesses and social dysfunctions. The absence of true fathers in the house of the Lord has also led to many serious dysfunctions in the body of Christ. So the last communication from the Old Testament addresses what is today a very serious issue. By being the last information of the Old Testament, this promise of Elijah was taken seriously by all scribes and Pharisees. Even four hundred years later in Jesus' day, it was clearly known by all that "Elijah" must first come. And today, Orthodox Jews still put a chair out for Elijah at Passover—just in case he returns, as Malachi prophesied.

Jesus' disciples asked Him about this in Matthew 17:10–13:

> And His disciples asked Him saying, "Why then do the scribes say that Elijah must come first?" Jesus answered and said to them, "Indeed Elijah is coming first and will restore all things. But I say to you that Elijah has come already, and they did not know him but did to him whatever they wished. Likewise the Son of Man is also about to suffer at their hands." Then the disciples knew that He spoke to them of John the Baptist.
>
> —MATTHEW 17:10–13

Jesus validated the Jewish expectation that Elijah would come before their Messiah showed up. He also established that John the Baptist came in the "spirit of Elijah" (Luke 1:17) and also that there would be a future "coming of Elijah" that would precede His return. Jesus simplified Elijah's task down to the restoration of all things, which Peter also referred to in a sermon in Acts:

> That He may send you Jesus Christ, who was preached to you before, whom heaven must receive until the time of restoration of all things, which God has spoken by the mouth of all His holy prophets since the world began.
>
> —ACTS 3:20–21

That word *restoration—apokatastasis* in the original Greek text—is very powerful. It means "restoration of a true theocracy" and "restoration of original intent." The implications of this scripture are, of course, huge. Jesus is retained in heaven *until* Elijah's Revolution. Even as John the Baptist prepared the way for Jesus to come, the Elijah Revolution will prepare for His final return. We know John the Baptist's revolution didn't go far enough because it brought repentance but not a restoration of all things. His and Jesus' deaths, however, became the seeds for the coming restoration of all things that will precede Jesus' return. An original plan and design of God will triumph and will establish Him as Ruler of the nations. Exactly how that will look is debatable, but it clearly entails the crushing of Satan here on Earth before He returns for His bride.

THE UNTIL FACTOR

> The Lord said to my Lord, "Sit at My right hand, till I make Your enemies Your footstool."
>
> —MATTHEW 22:44

This passage is intended to shape our eschatology. Together with Acts 3, it gives us critical information about God's timing—"the until factor." In essence, the Father says to the Son, "Once You have purchased redemption for mankind, You will sit at My right hand. You will have done Your part on Earth 'till I make Your enemies Your footstool.' You will remain up here as the Head, and Your body on

Earth will crush Your enemies. The last generation will be the 'foot' generation and will rule on Earth over Your enemies. Until they do so, You are not going back to rescue, rapture, save, or anything else. Your body, in fact, will not be a beautiful bride until she has accomplished this crushing of Satan."

The restoration of all things and making Satan a footstool are both the same work. One makes room for the other, and all of it precedes Jesus' return. Just to make sure this passage didn't get undersold, the Holy Spirit had it placed in Psalm 110, Mark 12:36, Luke 20:43, Hebrews 1:13 and 10:13, as well as in this Matthew 22:44 text!

Elijah will first come and raise up that which will destroy the spirit of Baal and the spirit of Jezebel here on Earth. We are going to take on the false prophet and the beast, and we're going to annihilate both of them. When they are crushed, we will come to the Lord and say, "The kingdoms of this world have become the kingdoms of our God" (Rev. 11:15). We will present the nations of the world to the Lord as His possessions. They will be the dowry that the Father is providing for us to present to the Bridegroom. Lovesick for His bride, Jesus will no longer be able to restrain Himself and will burst through the clouds to come sweep us off our feet. Our Prince Charming will come on a white horse to take us away. (See Revelation 19:11.) But He's not coming for a lazy, spoiled prostitute—He's coming for an overcoming, conquering, love-motivated bride who has made herself ready by fulfilling her mission. (See Revelation 19:7.) The Elijah Revolution is the catalyst for all of these things.

 SEVEN MANIFESTATIONS OF ELIJAH

1. Prophet

The Elijah Revolution will restore the prophet's ministry and prophetic gifts to their proper place. (See 1 Corinthians 14:1.) Acts 2:17 tells us, "And it shall come to pass in the last days, says God, that I will pour out of My Spirit on all flesh; Your sons and daughters shall prophesy, Your young men shall see visions, Your old men shall dream dreams…and they shall prophesy. The outpouring of the last days is an outpouring specifically of everything prophetic."

2. Intercessor

The Elijah Revolution will sweep through the church and prioritize prayer to the point that we will truly be called "a house of prayer for all nations" (Isa. 56:7). We will move beyond "second heaven" intercession, where we are overly conscious of the dark forces and their strategies, and we will step into "third heaven" intercession, where we go into heaven, see the counsel of God, and release His decrees on Earth—thus bringing the will of God "on earth as it is in heaven" (Matt. 6:10).

3. Exposer of Jezebel

Jezebel manifests as a religious spirit, as a spirit of seduction, or as some combination of both. The Revolution will completely remove the spirit's cloaking device that allows it to hide. Revelation 2:20 tells us that "she calls herself a prophetess" and hides in God's house. By the power of the Holy Spirit, Elijah revolutionaries will expose her.

4. Decimator of Baal's Prophets

Jezebel is a servant of Baal, the god over abortion, homosexuality, divorce, self-mutilation, and mammon. (Wall Street's term *the bull market* comes from the Baal bull.) The Elijah Revolution will make an open show of the superiority of God over Baal with Mount Carmel-like confrontations. Mardi Gras descends from Baal worship and is one reason that New Orleans was left exposed to great devastation. One year before Hurricane Katrina devastated New Orleans and the Gulf coast, I wrote in my prophetic newsletter warning that we as a nation have an altar of Baal from Mobile to New Orleans, and that the next hurricanes would decimate them. It was very specific to New Orleans and Biloxi. Baal *must* be confronted and *must* be defeated. This will be a significant work of the Elijah Revolution.

5. Practitioner of the Supernatural

Elijah comes as the antidote to the religious spirit—that which has a form of godliness but no power (2 Timothy 3:5). Religion has a spiritual look but no substance or power. The Elijah Revolution will usher in a major healing revival everywhere it goes and will demonstrate the power of our God. Elijah revolutionaries will walk in unprecedented power and presence of the Lord. Through their words alone, they will cancel droughts, plagues, and adverse weather. Supernatural experiences will be their "bread," and they will demonstrate the truth that "greater is He that is in me than he that is in the world" (1 John 4:4). They will step into the greater works that Jesus promised us (John 14:12). Our promised land is walking on water, walking through buildings, being supernaturally transported, raising the dead, feeding thousands with very little, healing quadriplegics, casting out demons, turning water in wine, finding gold in a fish's mouth—*and greater!*

6. Eliminator of Ambiguity

The Elijah Revolution tsunami will sweep through and confront those who "falter between two opinions" (1 Kings 18:21). God will evidence Himself so powerfully that it will allow many who have faltered in double-mindedness to focus on what—and *who*—truth is. We will even see physical manifestations of "the God who answers by fire" (1 Kings 18:24), and there will be an explosion of testimonials like those described in 1 Kings 18:39: "Now when all the people saw it, they fell on their faces; and they said, the LORD, He is God! The LORD He is God!" They had been faltering between two opinions until they saw an Elijah demonstration.

7. Anointer of the Double Portion

Elijah not only did tremendous things in his generation; he also released even greater things to the next generation. His successor, Elisha, received a double portion of his spirit. In fact, he performed exactly twice as many recorded miracles as Elijah did. Likewise, our ceiling is to be our children's floor. They are to start building where we leave off, particularly in prophetic anointing and the anointing to restore all things. Every nation has a redemptive destiny, and the Lord is urging us to ask Him for the nations as an inheritance (Psalm 2:8). The generation that is produced from the Elijah Revolution will have unprecedented faith to prophesy to, over, and for nations and will see it as a small thing to believe that a nation can be taken in a day. It was Elisha who finally anointed Jehu as king, and it is he who finally destroyed Jezebel. The proper, timely restoration of the apostolic ministry is the key that will finally deal Jezebel her deathblow. We currently have many premature and immature manifestations of apostles because the prophetic hasn't yet been fully established. Jehu represents the apostolic role, and until Jehu is in place, Jezebel will be able to operate at some level or another. Jezebel's final removal from the high places will be enforced through true apostles. The Elijah Revolution prepares the way for all this to happen.

COULD THE ACTUAL ELIJAH COME?

It is reasonable to speculate that we may see Elijah literally return at some point. Why? First, Scripture actually says he will come before the Lord's return, and it doesn't bother to specify whether this is something "in the spirit of Elijah," like John the Baptist, or Elijah himself. Second, Hebrews 9:27 says, "It is appointed unto men once to die, but after this the judgment" (KJV). Elijah has yet to die, as he was taken to heaven in a whirlwind. If he is appointed to die, both he and Enoch (and possibly Moses, depending on what really happened to his disappeared body) could be sent back to Earth. Two of those three could be the witnesses referred to in Revelation 11:3. These two, it says, have the power to release fire from their mouth, to keep rain from falling, to turn water into blood, and to strike the earth with plagues. These descriptions fit the ministries of Moses and Elijah perfectly.

That could be why these men were the two who appeared with Jesus at His transfiguration. Peter's comments are interesting: "Lord it is good for us to be here; if you wish, let us make here three tabernacles: one for You, one for Moses, and one for Elijah" (Matt. 17:4). To Peter, Moses and Elijah seemed to be in as natural a state as Jesus was. Apparently he even thought it would make sense for them to be coming to live the rest of their lives. For all we know, Moses and Elijah could be regular visitors on planet Earth, as we are not aware of what restrictions they may or may not have—an early appearance of the two witnesses that Revelation says will greatly stress the rebellious inhabitants of Earth. If so, that would leave Enoch as something of a "wild card" to pleasantly surprise us in many ways. The way history ends is going to have more exciting twists and turns and be much better than the best movie Hollywood has ever produced.

Whether the actual, natural Elijah returns or not is a matter of speculation, as Scripture isn't clear about it. But you may want to keep an eye out for him. Having never tasted death, he has a dual passport to heaven and Earth. Either way, the Elijah Revolution will come. With or without him, a movement in the body of Christ will operate in the spirit of Elijah—*before* the Lord returns.

Thrust Into the Promised Land

THE ELIJAH REVOLUTION tsunami will thrust us upon the nations and into our promised land. A parallel in the book of Joshua serves to give us even more insight into what will take place. As we explore this book, we'll see that it's more than inspirational; it's also strategically relevant.

Joshua 3 describes Israel's crossing the Jordan River:

> Then Joshua rose early in the morning, and they set out from Acacia Grove and came to the Jordan, he and all the children of Israel, and lodged there before they crossed over. So it was, after three days, that the officers went through the camp; and they commanded the people, saying, "When you see the ark of the covenant of the LORD your God, and the priests, the Levites, bearing it, then you shall set out from your place and go after it. Yet there shall be *a space between you and it, about two thousand cubits* by measure. Do not come near it, that you may know the way by which you must go, *for you have not passed this way before.*"
>
> —JOSHUA 3:1–4, EMPHASIS ADDED

YOU HAVE NOT PASSED THIS WAY BEFORE

The coming tsunami will project us into a place we've never been before. Israel had lived in bondage to Egypt for four hundred years. They had also lived forty years in the wilderness. The one place they had never yet been was the place of their ultimate destiny—the Promised Land. Everything would be different in this place, and they would see and experience things that they had never before seen or experienced. For that reason, they were instructed to be ready for the unexpected—"you have not passed this way before."

This, of course, is an important message for us today. The Elijah Revolution cross over will take us into dimensions we have *never* seen before. This means we will not be able to say things like, Oh, yeah, this is like the Protestant Reformation; This is like the Great Awakening in Jonathan Edwards's day; or This is like the Welsh Revival—or even the Azusa Street Revival, the healing movement of the forties and fifties, or the Jesus movement of the sixties. There will be nothing to compare it to because God isn't trying to get us to relive history. The dimensions of the Revolution will be very different than the past.

Israel was used to circling in the wilderness and remembering every place they arrived at from the last time they were there. Every experience carried some degree of a déjà vu factor. Now, however, they were told to fasten their seatbelts—"for you have not been this way before."

CUBITS OR YEARS?

Israel was told to follow the ark of the covenant—the vessel of the presence of God—by two thousand cubits. Israel would not dare enter the land without coming in behind this holy presence. Two thousand cubits is a very prophetic measure that gives us some insight into the specific timing of our crossing over.

Jesus Christ would become a prophetic fulfillment of the ark—the vessel of the presence of God—as He was God in the flesh and in Him dwelt the fullness of the Godhead. (See Colossians 2:9.) Interestingly, we are now about two thousand years after Jesus made His appearance on Earth. Prophetically, that seems to give us a symbolic timing element for our revolutionary crossover into the promised land.

Hosea 6:2 also lends support to this possibility: "After two days He will revive us; in the third day He will raise us up, and we shall live in His sight." We are told in 2 Peter 2:8 that with the Lord, a day is as a thousand years. Using these mathematics, "after two days" translates to "after two thousand years." That's when He'll revive us.

Our generation is the appointed time for crossing over—for the

Elijah Revolution revival. We will enter dimensions we have never entered before because He will revive us and raise us up. The Hebrew word for *revive* is *chayah,* which means "to live prosperously, to restore, to revive from sickness, from discouragement, from faintness, from death." Contrary to the belief of many, these blessings are a hope we can latch on to right here, on Earth, right now!

The reason He is reviving us is not so He can rapture us before the enemy wipes us out. Rather, He is reviving us to raise us up. The Hebrew *quwm* means "to arise and become powerful, to fulfill, to rise up and impose." Before He raptures us, or takes us away, He's going to make us powerful. Before He bursts through the clouds to come get us, we're going to fulfill our mission and assignment. That mission and assignment is to impose the desires of heaven on Earth. We will fulfill Jesus' prophetic prayer of Matthew 6:10—that God's will be done here on Earth as it is in heaven. In other words, to establish heavenly reality before He comes.

We're very familiar with the future reign of our King, but He also has a present and ever-increasing reign. Isaiah 9:7 tells us that "of the increase of His government...There will be no end." His government will always be on the increase—here on Earth—as we arise and impose the will of God. The victims of our "imposing" are not people; people will benefit greatly. The victims will be demonic powers and principalities. All else will take care of itself as we accomplish this assignment.

THE PROMISED LAND IS THE NATIONS

Israel did not own land, nor did they possess cities or nations, while they were in the wilderness for those forty years. They were survivalists with a defensive mentality. Their minds and spirits had been shut down to their potential by four hundred years of servitude in Egypt. They had an ingrained poverty spirit brought on by a history of just trying to survive. Though God was supernaturally able to extract them from Egypt in just one day, it took Him forty years to extract Egypt from them. In fact, only two, Joshua and Caleb, were taken all the way from Egypt to the Promised Land. All others died in their

not their children!

31

unbelief on the way. Once they had crossed the Red Sea, the Promised Land could have been theirs in a matter of days, from a geographical standpoint. Yet it was forty years before the people of Israel finally crossed the Jordan and began to take the nations that were promised to them.

It's important that we understand that displacing these nations was the original promise God gave Moses from the burning bush of Exodus 3.

> The LORD said, "I have surely seen the oppression of My people who are in Egypt, and have heard their cry because of their taskmasters, for I know their sorrows. So I have come down to deliver them out of the hand of the Egyptians, and to bring them up from that land to a good and large land, to a land flowing with milk and honey, to the place of the Canaanites and the Hittites and the Amorites and the Perizzites and the Hivites and the Jebusites."
>
> —EXODUS 3:7–8

THE WILDERNESS WAS NEVER PROMISED TO ISRAEL

This point is extremely relevant for us today. The wilderness was *never* promised to Israel. We too, have lived a Christian wilderness experience for the last two thousand years, but this was never God's original intent. His purpose is spelled out in Exodus 3. To paraphrase, He says: "I've seen the cry and the oppression of My people and I don't like it. I'm not a sadistic God. My heart is to bless those who are called by My name with as much blessing as they can handle without self-destructing. I have a good and large land for them—a land that flows with milk and honey. I have unlimited abundance and unlimited favor for them there, and it is my heart to give it to them."

The sneaky part of this promise is what He added as a throw-in. This place of promise was currently dominated by the Canaanites, Hittites, and a lot of other *-ites*. More details on them would come later, but the initial deal was laid out at the burning bush: Take the land of the nations of the land—and boy, do I have incomparable blessings for you there.

THE MANNA WAS NEVER GOD'S ORIGINAL PLAN

Just as the wilderness itself was never Israel's promised destiny, neither was manna part of God's ultimate purpose. Though we sing songs about manna from heaven and romanticize the miracle of bread falling from the sky, it's important to remember that God had always promised something better. He never told Moses or Israel, "I will provide manna from heaven every morning." No, He promised milk and honey. That's why the manna stopped on the day after they first ate of the produce of the land (see Joshua 5:12). Manna was a wafer-like substance that had only a hint of honey flavoring to it. The promise was a land that *flowed* with honey. God provided in the desert a sample of what would be available without measure if they pressed forward. He was only whetting their appetites for what He really wanted to give them. These emergency rations would have been unnecessary if not for Israel's stubborn unbelief. In His goodness, God provides for us, even when we live below His calling on our lives.

To this point in history, we mainly have wilderness testimonies about how the Lord intervened at the last moment and provided for a basic need. "I was facing eviction from my house but somebody gave us a check out of nowhere," for example, or "My phone was about to be cut off, but then the Lord came through." These are truly testimonies of God's goodness, and it is important for them to be told. But it is still far below what God has had in mind for us.

An example of a promised land testimony, as opposed to a wilderness testimony, would be, "Our twelve-year-old went to the local hospital and laid hands on the building itself—and suddenly, one by one, all the sick came out of the hospital totally healed!" It is the same grace and power, but in an extremely higher measure: greater grace and greater power, accessed by greater faith. This kind of testimony of God's power is what the Elijah Revolution will begin to reveal.

WATER FROM THE ROCK WAS NEVER GOD'S ORIGINAL PLAN

As with manna, we love to sing about and be inspired by the water that came out of a rock. But, like manna, this blessing was never promised to Israel either. If God's people had been obedient to His intentions, there would never have been a need for water from the rock. It was an emergency miracle that shouldn't have been necessary:

> The Lord your God is bringing you into a good land, a land of brooks of water, of fountains and springs, that flow out of valleys and hills.
>
> —DEUTERONOMY 8:7

> The land which you cross over to possess is a land of hills and valleys, which drinks water from the rain of heaven.
>
> —DEUTERONOMY 11:11

All along, God spoke to Israel of a land that had no drought, a land that flowed abundantly with every kind of water. There were brooks, fountains, and springs, and if that wasn't enough, there was plenty of rain from heaven. It was truly a "you have never passed this way before" kind of land.

God provides the emergency kind of revivals we thirst for—our water in the desert—to save the church from being irrelevant. But in the promised land, the atmosphere of revival is constant and ever increasing. It's in the last days that He pours out His Spirit without measure.

In that context, consider how enlightening—and ironically tragic—it is that Moses sinned and forfeited his entrance into the Promised Land because of his frustration with Israel at the site of a water-from-a-rock miracle. Every time a miracle of emergency provision took place, it was yet another reminder that Israel was a stiff-necked and unbelieving people who were not where they were supposed to be. They were in need of an Elijah Revolution to understand their call and destiny—just like we are.

Seven Nations
Greater and Mightier

When the LORD your God brings you into the land which you go to possess, and has cast out many nations before you, the Hittites and the Girgashites and the Amorites and the Canaanites and the Perizzites and the Hivites and the Jebusites, *seven nations greater and mightier than you.*"

—DEUTERONOMY 7:1, EMPHASIS ADDED

G OD HAD BEEN speaking extensively to Moses and Israel about this Promised Land He had planned for them. In Deuteronomy 7, He let them in on a little secret. The nations He was sending them to defeat were "greater and mightier" than they were. In essence, He was saying, "I have this place of incredible blessing for you, a large land, a good land, a land that flows milk and honey—but the enemy that is presently there is impossible for you to overcome. They are bigger and stronger than you."

Wow. That takes the air out of the balloon a little, doesn't it? Israel had been promised abundant living at every level, but the promise comes in spite of a seemingly insurmountable obstacle. For us, this promise translates into abundant living in body, soul, and spirit; abundance in the fruit of the Holy Spirit. It is an Isaiah 60:1 phenomenon—great darkness on the nations, but His glory coming upon us. There is abundance of provision, not so we can show off our Jaguars and Rolexes, but to finance the massive final harvest.

The abundance is in the power and presence of God. While plagues ravage the world, He will be very present in our midst as the Lord who heals us.

This is what our future holds as we cross over in this Elijah Revolution tsunami. As we target cities and nations—remember His invitation to "ask of Me and I will give You the nations for Your inheritance" (Psalm 2:8)—He promises to pour out what we've been trying to get in the wilderness.

That's why the prosperity gospel taught by many is so misguided. Outside the context of taking the nations, it's as foolish as Israel expecting milk and honey in the desert. The wilderness and the promise of abundance don't go together. There's a limit on the power He'll release to us if our goal is just to make the wilderness more livable. The greater works promised by Jesus, the greater provision, and the greater peace and joy all come as we embrace the impossible task of taking nations. This is the gospel of the kingdom as opposed to the gospel of salvation. He doesn't just want souls; He's coming to enforce His rule over all of creation.

THE GOSPEL OF THE KINGDOM VERSUS THE GOSPEL OF SALVATION

This entire crossing over of Jordan can be seen as another kind of crossing over—from understanding only the gospel of salvation to now understanding the gospel of the kingdom.

The message of salvation, experientially, is our crossing the Red Sea out of Egypt. The Red Sea speaks prophetically of the blood of Jesus that makes a way for us to be saved from our flesh and the devil. Through the blood of Jesus, the bondage of Egypt is broken, and as we are in Christ (the Red Sea) we are free from our oppressors. If we are in Christ, the enemy (Pharaoh and his men) has no access to us and will be destroyed if he follows us. It's the wonderful truth of the redemptive work Christ did on the cross. It's the message of knowing Jesus Christ as Savior. When we take only that message to the world, we tend to be concerned only with "souls, souls, souls." But crossing the Red Sea alone doesn't get us into the Promised Land.

The gospel of the kingdom includes the gospel of salvation, but it goes well beyond that. Crossing the Jordan represents a second application of the Cross. It's a further revelation of what Jesus' death accomplished. Jesus is not just Savior, He is also Lord. He not only paid the price for every soul that ever lived, He also paid the price for all of creation to be redeemed. He doesn't consider His creation to be disposable; it, too, is crying out for redemption. (See Romans 8:22.) When He created the Earth and seas, Scripture says, "God saw that it was good" (Genesis 1:10). We need to establish a proper theology of the earth. If not, we will never be able adjust our thinking to understand the gospel of the kingdom.

Consider what the Bible says about the earth:

Genesis 1:1—God is Creator of the earth.

Genesis 1:10—God sees that what He created is good.

Genesis 1:26—The Trinity commune together and give man dominion over all.

Genesis 1:28—God instructs humanity to "subdue the earth" and to have dominion "over every living thing."

Genesis 6:13—Because of the violence of man, the Lord says that He will "destroy" Earth. (That word is important because many later misinterpret *destroy* as *obliterate*, when the word actually means "batter, ruin, injure." As we see even in the Noah account, it was a judgment, not a wiping out of the world.)

Genesis 14: 19—Melchizedek says that God is "Possessor of heaven and earth."

The Hebrew word for *possessor* is *ganah*, which means "He who created, bought, acquired, or redeemed."

Numbers 14:21—The Lord tells Moses that not only is there a real Promised Land, a different dimension of life, but that as surely as He, the Lord, lives, "all the earth shall be filled with the glory of the Lord."

Joshua 3:13—As they are about to cross over to their Promised Land, Joshua tells the people that God is "Lord of all the earth."

1 Samuel 2:8—It says that even "the pillars of the earth are the Lord's."

Psalm 21:10—The Lord says He will destroy the wicked from the world.

Psalm 24:1—"The earth is the Lord's and all its fullness, The world *and* those who dwell therein" (emphasis added). He extends His ownership over everything He created *and* the people of it.

Psalm 37:9—Evildoers will be cut off from the earth, but those who wait on the Lord "shall inherit the earth."

Psalm 37:11—"The meek shall inherit the earth."

Psalm 37:22—"For those blessed by Him shall inherit the earth, But those cursed by Him shall be cut off."

This is not an exhaustive list of what Scripture says about God and the earth, but it is enough to establish a proper theology on the topic. God created the earth and its people, and together they constitute His creation. He saw everything He made and liked it, calling it "good." The heavens are the Lord's, the earth is the Lord's, the people of the earth are the Lord's. *He is not willing to lose anything.* That He values the earth is clear; it is the inheritance He wishes to give those who please Him. It isn't just the disposable nest where He placed man. The fact that He made man from the dust of the ground makes an irrevocable connection between humanity and the earth. The long-term inheritance of the earth is a goal to be desired. If the meek and the righteous "inherit the earth," it can't be a temporary inheritance that will last only until God burns it up. The only destruction ever coming to the earth is a cleansing destruction, not an obliterating destruction. God does not offer us something as an inheritance to then take it away.

God is so committed to Earth that He assures Moses that "as surely as He lives," the earth will be filled with His glory. Humans are the apple of His eye, but He loves and cherishes *everything* He created. Some dimension of restoration is coming for all He has made. God is an environmentalist. He doesn't prioritize Earth over His love for those created in His image, but it's still important to Him. We may have a bad political reaction to this topic if we hold an erroneous concept that the earth is disposable. Rapture politics has conditioned the church not to be concerned about the rest of creation. The Elijah Revolution will change this.

> The creation itself also will be delivered from the bondage of corruption into the glorious liberty of the children of God
> —ROMANS 8:21

Why would God care about something that doesn't have a soul? Because the rest of His creation still carries enough of His DNA to look to Him for deliverance and redemption. When He speaks, mountains and trees respond to Him. When He calls, oceans and seas react. In the days of Sodom and Gomorrah, the land itself lifted its cry to the Lord because of the cities' sin. We must grow in our understanding of the connection between God and *all* of His creation.

THE GREAT COMMISSION

> Go, therefore and make disciples of all the nations, baptizing them in the name of the Father and of the Son and of the Holy Spirit.
> —MATTHEW 28:19

With a proper theology of Earth, we can begin to better understand our commission. We can then develop a proper theology of the nations. Proper theology in these two areas give us a basis for understanding the gospel of the kingdom.

The Great Commission was to "make disciples of all nations." It was not to "make disciples of all souls." God is interested in the *nations*—a word mentioned over three hundred times in the Scriptures. Most of the Old Testament prophets prophesied to nations or cities; their blessings and/or curses were given on a citywide or nationwide basis. The nations themselves each have a destiny and an identity in the eyes of the Lord. He loves nations, and He loves cities.

More than knowing *why* He cares so much for the earth and nations, it's important simply to know that He *does*. Jesus made it clear that He came first for "the lost house of Israel" (Matthew 15:24)—for a nation.

When He wept in Luke 13:34, His cry was for "Jerusalem, Jerusalem"—for a city. Haggai 2:7 calls Him "the desire of the nations." Whether we understand it or not, He is jealous over entire countries. His zeal is to have them under His reign. That's the gospel of the kingdom.

The Bible is full of references to God's desire for the kingdoms of the earth. Here are a few that will help us begin to develop a proper theology of the nations:

Genesis 18:18—"Abraham shall surely become a great and mighty nation, and all the nations of the earth shall be blessed in him."

Psalm 2:8—"Ask of Me, and I will give You The nations for Your inheritance, And the ends of the earth for your possession."

Psalm 22:28—"For the kingdom is the LORD's, And He rules over the nations."

Psalm 47:3—"He will subdue the peoples under us, And the nations under our feet."

Jeremiah 1:10—"See, I have this day set you over the nations and over the kingdoms, To root out and to pull down, To destroy and to throw down, To build and to plant."

Hebrews 11:33—Speaking of the heroes of faith, it says that "through faith [they] subdued kingdoms."

Revelation 2:26—"And he who overcomes…to him I will give power over the nations."

God's relentless quest for the nations climaxes in Revelation 11:15:

Then the seventh angel sounded; And there were loud voices in heaven, saying, "The kingdoms of this world have become the kingdoms of our Lord and of His Christ, and He shall reign forever and ever!

Revelation 22, the last chapter in the Bible, then reveals the tree of life in heaven:

And the leaves of the tree were for the healing of the nations.

—REVELATION 22:2

This was Jesus' focus when He told of the end days:

> All the nations will be gathered before Him, and He will separate
> them one from another, as a shepherd divides his sheep from his
> goats. And He will set the sheep on His right hand, but the goats
> on the left.
>
> —MATTHEW 25:32–33

Regardless of when this time period may be, it's clear that a most interesting division or separation is taking place. Entire nations are separated into blessing or cursing. Perhaps you're asking yourself, *You mean I could be judged according to what my nation is doing—and not just what I'm doing?* The answer is *yes*.

Let me clarify: your entrance into heaven is very personal and is determined solely by your personal confession of faith in Jesus and His blood on the cross. You will, however, partake of a coming blessing or curse that relates to the direction your nation goes. This is by God's design so that you'll live in the gospel of the kingdom instead of just the gospel of salvation. He has given us authority over the nations, so there is a great price to pay when we don't exert that authority. The Elijah Revolution will wake us up to kingdom thinking.

History won't conclude, then, until Matthew 24:14 is fulfilled: "This gospel of the kingdom will be preached in all the world as a witness to all the nations, and then the end will come." All nations will have to hear and see—to witness is to see—this gospel of the kingdom before Jesus returns. The gospel of saving souls will not suffice—it's the gospel of the kingdom that must get out. That means the message of His Lordship over everything must be followed by a demonstration of His Lordship over everything. There will have to be at least one "sheep nation" before He calls all nations into judgment. The sons and daughters of the kingdom, of at least one nation, will enter their promised land and evict nations "greater and mightier" than they are. May many, many nations be so won by the children of the King.

THE SEVEN MOUNTAINS

Let's go back to the opening scripture of this chapter. In Deuteronomy 7, the Lord begins to tell Moses again about the Promised Land. It's the passion of the Lord's heart for His people. He does not want them in the desert. He does not want to give them emergency rations (manna). He does not want to refresh them with emergency water from a rock. He has *so* much more for them. He is constantly telling Moses about this good and large land He has for His people. It has always been the original intent of God's heart to bless with this place.

But in verse 1, He finally lays out the fact that these nations they were to rule and dispossess are "seven nations greater and mightier than you." He needed to reveal this before they saw their enemies so they would be prepared. He tells Israel:

> "If you should say in your heart, 'These nations are greater than I; how can I dispossess them?—you shall not be afraid of them, but you shall remember well what the LORD your God did to Pharaoh and to all of Egypt...So shall the LORD your God do to all of the peoples of whom you are afraid...You shall not be terrified of them; for the LORD your God, the great and awesome God, is among you. And the LORD your God will drive out those nations before you little by little...But the LORD your God will deliver them over to you, and will inflict defeat upon them until they are destroyed.
>
> —DEUTERONOMY 7:17–23

What the Lord was saying, in essence, was that it's easy to build a Great Commission theology around doubt and unbelief. It's more comfortable to embrace the ways of the wilderness—in other words, to desire to fall back on a salvation-only gospel that says once you've gotten your pass into heaven, you're all done (except for waiting for Him to take you by death or rapture, whichever comes first). God warned His people not to be terrified by the assignment because they would surely accomplish the mission if they committed to it. He assured them of victory and promised to perform whatever was necessary—with the same power that defeated Pharaoh and brought them out of Egypt. They just needed to be convinced that He had promised a better day for them.

The taking of the Promised Land is to be prophetically applied to our generation. It's a future event we can look forward to. How do we know that? Because that's how Isaiah described it:

> Now it shall come to pass in the latter days, That the mountain of the LORD's house, Shall be established on the top of the mountains, And shall be exalted above the hills; And all nations shall flow to it. Many people shall come and say, "Come and let us go up to the mountain of the LORD...He will teach us His ways.
> —ISAIAH 2:2–3

This passage speaks of a coming day when we would cross over Jordan as an Elijah Revolution tsunami—a day when the Lord's mountain of power and authority would be established above all other mountains and hills. These latter days are described in terms of something that has never taken place. As Joshua 3:4 says, "You have not passed this way before." The timing is about two thousand years after Jesus showed up on Earth. At this time, God will exalt those who are willing to believe Him for the impossible, and nations will flow to God's kingdom, saying "teach us His ways."

World systems are presently collapsing one by one and will continue to do so. Their "mountains" are failing, thus readying them to look to the only mountain of hope. This is not just a personal hope that individuals are looking for—i.e., the gospel of salvation—but a comprehensive hope that even entire nations can come under the rule and the glory of God.

THE SEVEN MOUNTAIN REVELATION

Over the last couple of years, I've begun speaking in several countries of the "crossing over" of Joshua 3 and Isaiah 2. I've shared that the mountains were the infrastructural columns of our societies—that it's the Lord's plan to raise His people up to take every social, economic, and political structure of our nations. I relate how history itself demonstrates that no nation is taken through revival alone. I explain that a gospel of salvation has never been comprehensive enough to see entire nations brought to the Lord. We must begin to change the way we think so that the Lord can begin to raise us to places of influence where we can truly be the light of our nations. (See Isaiah 60:3.)

The Lord even gave me a "seven-mountain revelation" of the seven structures that He is coming to take over. These mountains are: media, government, education, economy, religion, celebration of arts and entertainment, and family and social services.

Recently I heard a message by pastor, teacher, prophet, and personal coach Lance Wallnau called "The Seven Mountain Strategy." He shared how Loren Cunningham of Youth With a Mission (YWAM) was once scheduled for a lunch meeting with Bill Bright, the now-deceased leader of Campus Crusade. As they were on their way to meet each other, the Lord separately gave both of them the same revelation—a "seven-mountain strategy." In this revelation, the Lord told them that there were seven mountains, or kingdoms, to take—seven mind-molders of society. The Lord instructed each of them to tell the other this message, along with an important promise: capture these mountains, and you'll capture the nation.

They were both amazed, naturally, that the Lord had given them the same message on a strategy for taking a nation for God. They each described seven shapers of culture that directly correlate to the seven mountains I've listed above—confirmation that God is revealing this strategy to the leaders of His people. This approach, of course, is a radically new concept for most Christians. We have long assumed that evangelistic crusades and mass conversions are the key to taking a nation (if the thought of taking a nation even occurred to us). We have ignored entire mountains, or sectors of society, because they're "of the devil." But the Lord is now saying, "You must take these mountains."

This revelation is an earthquake that the Lord is releasing into His body. The shock waves of the revelation are beginning to sweep through Christian society, creating the tsunami waters upon which the Elijah Revolution will coming crashing upon the nations. This transformational change has already begun in several countries, and I'm amazed at what the Lord is doing in some situations I'm involved with. I've had the privilege of speaking prophetically to presidents, congressmen, senators, and other politicians in several countries. I've seen doors miraculously open for me to take a team into a country's legislature and prophesy over fourteen congressmen and aides and lead five of them to the Lord—just in one visit. Far beyond what I can share in this book, I'm already seeing indisputable evidence of the Lord beginning to infiltrate and take levels and areas of society that previously seemed unreachable. The tsunami of grace has caused a higher water table that is reaching higher places—so that His light may rule over nations.

Over the next seven chapters I'll go through each of these mountains and share strategies for taking them. There will be both prayer points and action points. One of my primary goals is to put legs on this exciting revelation. That will be particularly important for college students who are still deciding what their major is, but it applies to every Christian in any field. Every mountain has a strategy attached to it that relates to the seven nations of Deuteronomy 7—Hittites, Girgashites, Amorites, Canaanites, Perizzites, Hivites, and Jebusites. Each enemy nation reveals clues about the current rulers of the mountains we must take. The strategy is part *prayer*, because if we miss the spiritual warfare component of this battle we will fail; and it's part *action*, because having prayed, we must then respond to the grace that is released. Our faith and works must go hand in hand.

God is looking for men and women of faith through whom He can accomplish the impossible. Taking these mountains is an impossible task through human strategies. The prophetic word must be the initial penetrator of every mountain's defenses. That's why this is an *Elijah* Revolution. God announces everything He does before He does it. (See Amos 3:7.) That's not just the protocol of heaven; the anointed, prophetic word actually captures the enabling power of heaven and releases it on Earth. This is a time for prophets to be released into the mountains to proclaim what's about to happen.

That proclamation becomes the runway on which the actual promise lands. As jets only land on runways, so too will the Lord land on the runways of prophetic declaration. This is a primary purpose of this book—to prophetically declare what is currently en route and beginning to crash upon the nations.

Hittites and the
Mountain of Media

T HE MOUNTAIN OF media is currently occupied almost entirely by evil forces. Because we have never recognized the value of taking media outlets for the kingdom, they have become major tools of the Enemy that we must rend out of his hands. He has lived almost unopposed on this mountain, and he has taken full advantage of its influence.

WHAT IS MEDIA?

For our purposes, *media* refers to the news outlets that report and establish the news. Therein lies the power of the media—they can actually create the news. They can turn a non-story into *the* big story and turn what should be huge stories into non-stories. Media outlets include television stations and networks, Web sites, newspapers, radio stations, and magazines.

WHO RULES THE MEDIA?

The first enemy nation mentioned in Deuteronomy 7 was the Hittites. This enemy specifically relates to the problems of the mountain of media. The word *Hittite* comes from the name *Heth*, which means "fear" or "terror," and these terrifying spirits are having a heyday being released over the air through the various news outlets. They are arguably causing more damage than the actual terrorists, who have little influence without media cooperation. Rampant news coverage of terrorism creates faintness of heart throughout the world. That it's such a twisted fear makes it particularly damaging and dangerous.

A disproportionate fear creates a false central battlefield. Fear of Satan, terrorism, disease, plagues, or war puts the hearts of men and women on the wrong battlefield and conditions them to respond out of ungodly fears. It's the fear of the Lord that is the beginning of wisdom. All other fears only serve to advance Satan's kingdom.

Bad news is Satan's specialty, and twisting news is his delight. His goal is to flood the airwaves with bad news, bringing the battle to his home field, where he can easily pick off the fearful and anxious. After constant exposure to terrifying news, he can then easily inject illness into our weakened immune systems. (The proliferation of bad news is known to physically affect the heart and the immune system.) Satan constantly sets scenarios that distract us from what should be the true battlefields. He uses the media to create infighting and division at all levels of our society.

One of the primary reasons that the Iraq conflict has been so difficult and protracted is because of the complicity of the mainstream media to erode our national willpower by accentuating the most terrifying and horrific news of the conflict. As a nation, we are by and large fighting terrorists *and* the media. Terrorism isn't effective without the cooperation, intentional or not, of media. Terrorism's goal is terror, and it needs a spokesman—and the spokesman is not Osama bin Laden. That role goes to Al-Jazeera, CNN, and so on. Bin Laden has no voice unless they agree to release whatever he spews out.

Media is perhaps the hardest enemy to deal with because they are mainlined into our computers and televisions, both at work and at home. Every day we hear or read multiple reports from Iraq, for example, on casualties and every other tragic turn of events. Media outlets rarely tell of the schools Americans have built or the people we have helped in so many different ways in Iraq. Yet they don't miss a chance to pump into the nation any bad report available. They do it so well and so consistently that we actually believe it's a truthful picture. They have created a battlefield and convinced us that's where we must act as a priority. As a result, we quickly ask all political candidates their thoughts on the war and base our vote on this artificial battlefield created by the demonic powers on the top of the media mountain. The reporters themselves actually mean to express some measure of journalistic altruism, but media's physical faces are, by and large, just unwitting pawns of this mountain's ruling enemy.

Meanwhile, more people will die by abortion in any major American city than will die from war or terrorism in Iraq. This means that it is exponentially more dangerous to be a baby in an American womb than to serve on the front lines in a war. We also experience more daily deaths in this nation from car wrecks, suicide, murder, AIDS, cancer, heart attacks, drug overdoses, and many other causes. More people die every day from miswritten doctor's prescriptions than in the Iraq conflict, yet that fact isn't even known by the nation at large. The Iraq conflict is the front-page story only because the Hittites, the media, have made it so—and, in the process, greatly handicapped our ability to actually deal with terror.

Who Is the King of the Hittites?

I believe Apollyon serves as the ruling spirit over the Hittites who presently occupy the top of the mountain of media. I also believe he is going to be evicted from his place of influence.

Apollyon means "destroyer" or "destruction," and that's exactly what he releases through his control of this mountain. Revelation 9 describes those under Apollyon as having "tails like scorpions" and "there were stings in their tails." Scorpions have forked tails—or, for our purposes, forked "tales." This description fits the work produced by many media outlets. They are twisting events and making them say something they are not saying. Their sting is in their tales. The liberal agenda is actually a twisted look at issues resulting in a twisted interpretation of what would be a solution. Because of this, the enemy's strategy is to fill the mountain with humanistic, liberal people who become his most unwitting pawns in releasing his venom.

The word *liberal* means different things to different people in many nations. In this book, *liberal* will refer to American liberalism that seeks to be free from God-ordained ethics and values, as revealed in the Bible. I'm referring to a worldview that exalts humanity and demotes God (or at least His relevance). God may be in the picture, but He is not properly centered, so the compass for a proper worldview is askew. Conservatism often does no better at putting God in the middle of life, but the values espoused by conservatives are generally more consistent with a biblical worldview. God "in the middle" means that He is the center of the universe and we orbit around Him. Liberalism, on the other hand, unwittingly puts humanity at the center of the universe, and *if* God exists, He orbits around us. He's defined by what makes sense to our rational minds. Liberals are not bad people; they are just people who have been deceived into embracing a de-prioritized view of God. Because of this deception, Satan's great desire is to fill the airwaves with them and unwittingly release his twisted tales and terror upon the nations through them.

As God's righteous judgments are made manifest, however, the world will increasingly know that it is He who rules the earth. Many are already asking, Is God trying to say something to us with all these hurricanes, earthquakes, and tsunamis? In the minds of many, God is by necessity being brought back into the center of life.

THE IMPORTANT ROLE OF EVANGELISTS

God is raising up a new breed of evangelists to take this mountain of media. The word *gospel* means "good news." An evangelist is someone anointed to bring good news. The best news, of course, is what Jesus' sacrifice on the cross accomplished, giving us access into heaven. That's the traditional understanding of an evangelist from the perspective of the gospel of salvation, and it's correct—but not complete. In the gospel of the kingdom, we've seen that our nations also have a "soul" that the Lord is after. Bad news conditions a soul to respond to satanic influences. Good news conditions a soul to respond to God because God is good.

There's an inherent value to good news that extends beyond just the message of salvation. Paul wrote:

> Whatever things are true, whatever things are noble, whatever things are just, whatever things are pure, whatever things are

> lovely, whatever things are of good report, if there is any virtue
> and if there is anything praiseworthy—meditate on these things.
> —PHILIPPIANS 4:8

This passage should be the guiding philosophy for anyone who feels led to take on the mountain of media. This is who the Lord will help and promote. The airwaves are to be filled with that which is true, that which is noble, that which is just, that which is pure, that which is lovely, that which is of a good report, that which is of virtue, and that which is praiseworthy. The Lord's school of journalism grows out of this passage. Any news network that incorporates these standards into its news reporting will begin to be lifted up to the top of the mountain by the Lord.

That doesn't mean it's wrong to report on a disaster or on a negative turn of events, or even on human mistakes and corruption. It does mean, however, that instead of endlessly replaying a disaster, the positive response to negative news can be highlighted. There is a redemptive, silver lining in every tragic event, an element of hope somehow connected to it. The airwaves must be filled with the kind of story angles that release hope.

We meditate on and are motivated by whatever is before our eyes. Because the kindness and goodness of the Lord leads to repentance (Romans 2:4), filling the airwaves with news and stories of nobility, truth, justice, virtue, and praiseworthy things can actually change the spiritual climate. (See Romans 2:4.) As the climate changes, there's an increased conductivity toward repentance. The end result will be that more souls will come to the Lord by our targeting the mountain of media than by targeting souls themselves. Good news conditions people's hearts to the One who is good.

LEVELS OF THE MOUNTAIN

As we read in Isaiah 2:2, the top of the mountain is where the Lord's house will be established. We are to take the whole mountain, but we will have strong grace upon us to reach the *top*. As we look next at the various levels and what they mean for us, remember that these are not precise categories but rather a generalization of spheres of influence.

The top of the mountain

This is where the principality Apollyon sits and from where he must be displaced. We can't only pray him down; we have to have the substitute ready and available. That's why taking a mountain requires prayer *and* action. This mountain needs to be occupied by Elijah revolutionaries who will report good news.

The top of the mountain is the part that penetrates into the "second heaven." (Note: The second heaven is where the remaining battle for earth takes place. Demonic powers have already been displaced from any third heaven authority. Their remaining power is only in what humans give them as we are deceived by their assault on our thought realm.) Whatever reigns in the second heaven will rule in the corporate thought realm, so winning the top of the mountain gives us power in the thought realm. The principle that "as a man thinks, so is he" also applies to nations (Prov. 23:7). That's why taking all the tops of these mountains also takes captive the thought life of a nation.

> The weapons of our warfare are not carnal but mighty in God for pulling down strongholds, casting down arguments and every high thing that exalts itself against the knowledge of God, bringing every thought into captivity to the obedience of Christ.
>
> —2 CORINTHIANS 10:4–5

We've somewhat understood the personal context of this passage, but there's also a corporate context. It's from the top of the mountains that we cast down the thoughts that exalt themselves against God.

The top of the mountain will always hold influence over millions of people in a trans-local capacity. In other words, whoever is influencing the minds of millions in some way occupies a position at the top. The behind-the-scenes financiers and decision-makers are obviously very key. Whoever sets the philosophical guidelines for the news reporting are the people with the real influence. The visible personalities may function as puppets if they don't have significant freedom of personal expression. FOX News, CNN, the BBC, the *New York Times,* Associated Press, *Time,* and similar high-profile outlets are examples of visible manifestations of the institutions positioned at the top of the mountain.

These places of influence involve demons, human institutions, and individuals. Obviously, not everyone at these organizations is bad, liberal, or demonic. Many Christians work in mainstream media, in fact, but they are compelled to work under current philosophical constraints of those media. A few may expose the hypocrisies of media—Sean Hannity operates in that role, for example—but we haven't yet seen the goal or even an accurate role model for what's to come. The result is a pervasive negative presence in most news organizations.

The middle of the mountain

The middle of the mountain is occupied by media outlets that are somewhat less influential. They reach thousands trans-locally rather than millions. Various newspapers, magazines, some news programs, special-interest national publications, and large-market local broadcast stations are among those halfway up the mountain. Institutions of higher education that train journalists would also fit here. Generally speaking, it's those with significant but not dominant influence. Though grace is given for the tsunami to reach the highest places, some will be called to occupy the mountain at this intermediate level. Elijah revolutionaries will need to be positioned at local news shows and newspapers that have widespread influence over certain geographic areas or social sectors.

The lower mountain

This level obviously reaches fewer people than the others. It could be mid- or small-market local news, specialty news programs, or magazines with lower circulation—influential, but not comparable to the top two levels. This level is about as much as Christians have had faith to reach—or even desired to reach. That's changing as the effects of the spiritual tsunami are felt.

WHAT THE BIBLE SAYS ABOUT NEWS

Before I quote a few scriptures on the subject, I want to reiterate the fact that news is not a minor issue. The news we *hear* and the news we *give* are both powerful conditioners of the human spirit. Defiled news defiles people, and noble news invigorates people. News that is properly presented extracts the redemptive message God is giving. God does not bring us hopeless, tragic news and just expect us to deal with it. He always seasons it with hope.

God shows us this model in the seven letters to the seven churches of the book of Revelation. His trademark presentation even of very stern, corrective warnings was done in a redemptive way. Jesus would first tell a church something positive—"you have tested those who say they are apostles and are not," for example, and "you have persevered…and have not become weary" (Rev. 2:2–3). Then He would deliver His central message, ie, the bad news: "Nevertheless, I have this against you that you have left your first love…Repent…or else I will come to you to…remove your lampstand" (Rev 2:4–5). The Lord then closed His message with another positive encouragement: "And you hate the deeds of the Nicolatians, which I also hate" (Rev. 2:6). His final word to the church is an uplifting promise: "To him who overcomes I will give to eat from the tree of life" (Rev. 2:7). The message comes as a divine "sandwich." The bread on each side is something positive or redemptive, while the meat of the message is actually very negative and serious.

The objective picture of the church at Ephesus—the example in the verses above—was that God was on the verge of extinguishing them because of their lack of love. Yet He couched it in amazing grace, while still bringing home the seriousness of the moment. The Lord knows the tremendous impact of news upon a person or group of people and that continual bad news with no redemptive angle will actually break a spirit. When some person or institution has a reporting platform, there's a tremendous responsibility to use that position of influence redemptively.

With that in mind, let's look at a few scriptures:

As cold water to a weary soul, So is good news from a far
country.

—PROVERBS 25:25

This passage is particularly interesting in light of United States's
battles in other nations such as Iraq and Afghanistan. If the effect of
good news on a nation's soul is refreshing like cold water, then we can
imagine what a constant stream of bad news does to the weary soul
of a nation. It would be like providing dust to someone who is thirsty,
and that's what U.S. citizens feel like after several years of fighting
terrorism—a battle we must fight in one way or another. The bad news
is a profoundly significant weapon that favors the terrorists.

Terrorists are for whatever destabilizes and engenders the most fear
and anxiety. Ninety percent of their success has come through media
reports. They have won no significant battle and are dying at a ratio
of more than ten to one compared to U.S. losses. Yet according to
the reports of a willing media, the U.S. is supposedly losing this war
because Americans can't stop Iraqis from killing each other. My point
is not to defend or condemn the war; it's that news has the power to
affect the psyche of individuals and even a whole nation. As believers
rise in prominence on this mountain of media, we are to understand
the godly philosophy of news and not collaborate in poisoning the
psyche of a nation.

How beautiful upon the mountains Are the feet of him who
brings good news, Who proclaims peace, Who brings glad
tidings of good things.

—ISAIAH 52:7

We can again see the heart of our Lord as it relates to bringing
news. Those who are called to take this mountain will have Isaiah 52's
"beautiful feet" to whatever degree they release good news, peace, and
hope—even when addressing issues that are inherently wrong and
negative. This isn't about deceiving people or covering up things that
need to be uncovered. It's making sure that the report has a redemptive end and leaves some hope as an aftertaste.

If you are a Christian who is (or plans to be) a member of the media, this is critical to understand. Your role on the mountain of media is always to try to release good news. We actually need to understand this point on an even broader scale as the church addresses issues of sin and corruption. Constant harping on abortion may serve only to further alienate opponents to the pro-life stance. Redemptive stories of those who chose not to have an abortion, however, or of those who have experienced God's forgiveness for an abortion will much more effectively win the hearts and minds of a nation.

> The Spirit of the Lord is upon Me, Because the Lord has anointed Me To preach good tidings to the poor; He has sent Me to heal the brokenhearted, To proclaim liberty to the captives, And the opening of the prison to those who are bound.
>
> —Isaiah 61:1

One of the new creative ways that the Lord is going to release His evangelists onto this mountain is by imparting the wisdom to transform reporting a news story into preaching "good tidings." Any journalist who can tell a story of heroism that incidentally portrays the heroic act as the outcome of a relationship with God is in fact preaching the good news. We need an army of evangelists who are "wise as serpents and harmless as doves" (Matt. 10:16), lying low and blending in, while having a kingdom agenda. As this army invades the mountain of media, they will begin to prepare the psyche of peoples and nations to receive from God.

> O, Zion, you who bring good tidings, Get up into the high mountain; O Jerusalem, You who bring good tidings, Lift up your voice with strength.
>
> —Isaiah 40:9

We could take this verse as a prophetic mandate from the Lord, that those who have the spirit of good news on them should "get up into the high mountains" and allow their voices to be heard. The story of David and Goliath reminds us how even one man can freeze an entire nation in fear through bad news. There's not a single biblical reference to Goliath ever having killed even one person. This giant was apparently vulnerable to a small stone from a slingshot, yet he employed the power of terror to neutralize any courage Israel might have had. David broke the power of his bad news with a declaration of good news. "This day the LORD will deliver you into my hand" (1 Samuel 17:46).

After his positive report, David easily dispensed with Goliath. Hundreds of formerly intimidated soldiers of Israel later became David's "mighty men," who could destroy not only giants but also entire armies. When we take the mountain of media and neutralize the bad news that flows down from it, we can begin using that mountain to release heaven on earth.

A MULTI-PRONGED APPROACH

There is no single, simple strategy for taking this mountain. One just needs to know that he or she is called to this mountain, and the Lord will begin to give wisdom and further strategy. Some will have the grace to do one thing and others the grace to do something else. We need a multi-pronged attack.

Christians need to begin rising up in journalism schools and shifting the philosophies of newspapers, or starting new papers that operate on godly principles. Networks like CNN and FOX can either be spiritually influenced or replaced by new alternatives that the Lord will raise up. He will release many creative ideas for the Internet, broadcast, and print media to those who are willing to identify media as their mountain and actually go for the top. Remember, He is releasing His tsunami both to displace that which is made of inferior building material *and* to establish His people on higher ground. The primary grace is for the top of the mountain and the displacement of Apollyon, the Hittites, and Goliath. The strategy is more spiritual than natural, so an Elijah journalist has to be spiritually girded for that kind of fight. To go up a mountain infiltrated by terrorists (the Hittites), fear and terror must not be allowed to rule in one's personal life. Whoever ascends this mountain should go with both a prayer strategy and an action strategy.

THE PRAYER STRATEGY

The prayer strategy should include several objectives. One is having a prayer covering and blessing over anyone currently on the mountain of media who is neutralizing the dark side. FOX News is well below the standard the Lord will raise, but by forcing a level of accountability on other news outlets, it's neutralizing an even greater darkness released from some of them.

Another prayer strategy is to pray for those news outlets and individuals we see carrying an unusual Apollyon anointing, that they would see the truth in Christ and turn from their ways. Al-Jazeera would be a case in point, as it has served as a Goliath for terrorism.

Other appropriate prayer strategies include praying the Lord's favor and help on those now starting up the mountain and for those yet to realize their calling in that area. Everything should be bathed and covered in prayer as our primary power weapon. "The weapons of our warfare are not carnal but mighty in God, for pulling down strongholds" (2 Cor. 10:4).

THE ACTION STRATEGY

Most, if not all, action strategies should be birthed in prayer. Substantial power could be released by going to the geographical stronghold of a spirit in media to pray or do prophetic acts. New York City is presently the stronghold site of Apollyon's influence. Atlanta is also important. Casting down the principality in the strongholds would be a global breakthrough. One needs to act within his or her bounds of faith and direction from God.

A primary action strategy is to choose a career in this field with a clear understanding of who you are and what you are to do. Christians have long served in this arena, but usually under the journalistic conditioning of the world. There is a difference between seeing yourself as a journalist who happens to be a Christian, and a son or daughter of the King on a specific mission. Now is the time for many who have felt the call to evangelism—and even prophesying or preaching—to realize that a media career is not only a viable fulfillment of that call, but also that Elijah revolutionaries will be specifically empowered to take this mountain. Part of the Revolution for the church is a better understanding that there is no such thing as "secular" work. There are only different mountains for us to function on. The whole world is now to be seen as our congregation. In these latter days, the mountain of the Lord's house will be exalted above the world's mountains, and, as Isaiah 2:2 indicates, nations will excitedly run to these new manifestations of heaven on earth.

Girgashites and the Mountain of Government

THE MOUNTAIN OF government, or politics, is a mountain that the Lord is beginning to position His children to invade and disciple. As with media, we've virtually given this mountain over to the world. Entire denominations have been known to prohibit their people from being involved with politics because of the corruption that always seems to infect it. The reason politics are considered "of the devil," of course, is because we have abandoned this mountain to him.

Because of the enemy's firm grip on this mountain, it's a very dangerous mountain to take if one is not spiritually prepared for it. Yet we *must* take it. The Elijah Revolution will begin to displace the forces of darkness from this mountain and establish righteous government on its top.

WHAT IS GOVERNMENT?

Government can have many applications, as there is government in many, many arenas. For our purposes, we are considering the political institutions that rule a land. They administrate civil righteousness and justice at multiple levels. Though it's a widespread field that extends far, the top of the mountain is occupied by a relatively small handful of people. In the United States, the president is the physical person at the top of the mountain, with senators and congressmen also high on our national mountain. Because our nation is the leader in the world at this time, it automatically places our national leader at the top of the world mountain of government.

WHO PRESENTLY RULES IN GOVERNMENT?

The second enemy nation mentioned in Deuteronomy 7 is the Girgashites. The name means "dwelling in clayey soil" and represents being motivated by earthy desires and ambitions. In essence it represents corruption brought on by the "pride of life" (1 John 2:16). The definition of *corruption* is "the impairment of integrity, virtue, or morality." This is what presently rules in politics and government.

All governments suffer from corruption, a built-in sabotage that guarantees their eventual implosion. The only government that will never have any corruption is the kingdom of God. Here on Earth, there will always be something less than a perfect government. We can (and should), however, insist on high ideals, principles, and individual character—people who can help manifest a form of government that is a blessing to a nation. Therefore, any attempt to establish a physical theocracy is ill-conceived. A government can potentially function as a virtual theocracy, but only as the individuals in power allow themselves to be puppets (i.e. servants) of the theocracy (God's rule and reign). The goal is to bring the influence of heaven to bear on whatever political machinery that exists.

WHO IS THE KING OF THE GIRGASHITES?

The mountain of government is perhaps the most important of the mountains because it can establish laws and decrees that affect and control every other mountain. Therefore, we find Lucifer himself entrenched on this mountain as the usurping "prince" over the nations. Whereas God's government is established through service and humility, Satan's government is established through manipulation and pride. Lucifer sits at the top of this mountain, where he specifically functions as the Antichrist. His role over the nations is to stir and raise up whatever would defeat the purposes of God on Earth. When he is firmly rooted in a nation, that nation will manifest the following Antichrist distinctives:

1. Working to destroy Israel
2. Working to destroy the next generation (abortion, wars, and plagues)
3. Working to destroy Christians
4. Working to suppress women or release Jezebels
5. Working to pervert sexual mores (homosexuality, adultery, etc.)

Each of these topics could be discussed in a separate book of their own, so we won't be able to develop them much deeper here. The point is that Lucifer tries to weave the seeds of these five distinctives into all aspects of governmental influence. He attempts to change and arrange laws, pacts, and agreements that will advance his agenda. And he still thinks he can succeed—which will just make the end result a little sweeter. Anyone attempting to climb this mountain of government must understand who is ruling and what he is looking to perform. The Girgashites of corruption serve his purposes because they condition people to be pawns of his master plan. The displacement of Lucifer is guaranteed by God, and nation by nation will be pulled out of his clutches:

> How you are fallen from heaven, O Lucifer, son of the morning! How you are cut down to the ground, You who weakened the nations! For you have said in your heart: "I will ascend into heaven, I will exalt my throne above the stars of God; I will also sit on the mount of the congregation On the farthest side of the north; I will ascend above the heights of the clouds, I will be like the Most High." Yet you shall be brought down to Sheol, To the lowest depths of the pit. Those who see you will gaze at you, And consider you saying, "Is this the man who made the earth tremble, Who shook kingdoms, Who made the world as a wilderness And destroyed its cities, Who did not open the house of his prisoners?
>
> —Isaiah 14:12–16

All who progress on this mountain of government will need to beware of the specific motivation brought out in this scripture. It's encapsulated in his statement, "I will ascend." Once your spirit has been penetrated by the prideful "I will ascend" motivation, you now carry the DNA of Satan—whether you're a Christian or not. Then the manipulation and pride work together. This mountain must therefore be taken by *practicing* Christians, not just *confessing* Christians. The antidote to Lucifer and his Girgashites of corruption is to walk in Matthew 20:28, "the Son of Man did not come to be served, but to serve, and to give His life a ransom for many."

This attitude must be the starting point for an Elijah revolutionary in politics. Humility and spiritual authority are required to take this mountain. That's the kind of person the Lord will raise up to displace the demons and their human puppets in the arena of government.

THE IMPORTANT ROLE OF APOSTLES

True apostles will play a unique role in the taking of this mountain. I have to say "true apostles" because most of those now calling themselves apostles aren't—and won't be any time in the future. It takes more than a Web site and a business card to become an apostle. It also takes more than having a network of churches under you. We have seriously dumbed down what an apostle is, and that has to change.

The church at Ephesus was praised for having "tested those who say they are apostles and are not, and have found them liars" (Rev. 2:2). Their self-promotion didn't disqualify them from being believers, and it didn't mean that they didn't have some kind of leadership position. It just meant that they weren't apostles and were therefore liars.

We have a good number of such liars bursting on the scene, thus muddying the waters for true apostles. That's not really a problem, because a basic trademark of a true apostle is that he doesn't mind not being recognized as one. The low profile helps his "cover"—he can access more grace from God (because God gives grace to the humble), and he's more overlooked as a target of the enemy that way. The temporary downside of less-than-apostles is that they are influencing many who want to properly honor true apostles.. They are serving as distracters for a season, but that will be remedied as God continues to shake His house.

An apostle is called and anointed to take the tops of the mountains. That anointing is not based on their charisma, their moneymaking ability, their networking, their personality type, their speaking skills, or any other naturally understood ability. It is authority with heaven based on a specific call—and then an obedient response to that call. It is moored in profound intimacy with the Godhead.

A quick look at the original twelve apostles should convince us that none of the natural qualities I've listed above define the role. Their natural gifts did not indicate the level of spiritual call upon their lives. Through them, we see a manifestation of God's divine strategy of choosing "nobodies" to turn the world upside down.

> For you see your calling brethren, that not many wise according to the flesh, not many mighty, not many noble, are called. But God has chosen the foolish things of the world...to put to shame the things which are mighty; and the base things of the world and the things which are despised God has chosen, and the things which are not, to bring to nothing the things that are, that no flesh should glory in His presence.
>
> —1 Corinthians 1:26–29

The Lord often hides His greater power and glory in unappealing wrapping paper. The apostles are a prime example. In fact, Jesus Himself is the perfect example of this dynamic. God came in the flesh and manifested Himself not through the household of Caesar, of Herod, of a centurion, or of any other prestigious leader; rather, He came hidden to a young maiden and then was born even more unpretentiously in a manger. Only wise men discovered Him, and it still takes wise men to discover the greater gifts of God.

Apostles are some of the greater gifts God gives us—often hidden, but anointed with power. And the greater of them will be some of the most unlikely individuals imaginable. In heaven they are very well known, mostly because of their cloak of humility. An apostle will have untold thousands of angels working with him because of the call upon his life, and many will be major territorial angels with a displacement anointing. They are the apostle's backup for taking mountaintops by displacing dark forces that are there.

Apostleship can be a virtually wasted gift here on earth if no one discovers the gift of God that is in him. Many apostles themselves may not even know that they are apostles, as the Lord may or may not reveal to them that identity. The title of apostle isn't important; it's the function and anointing that must be restored. A legitimate prophetic ministry in its proper place is supposed to call out and validate true apostles. Even as John the Baptist announced Jesus, so too do we need the prophetic voice to call forth and confirm apostles.

Jesus was the first legitimate apostle (see Hebrews 3:1), and He was the first to carry the proofs of an apostle. Everywhere Jesus went, apostolic phenomena took place. He confronted the top of the mountain in the spirit realm, so all hell and all heaven would break loose wherever He was. When He went into a city, the entire city would be confronted and shaken in some way. Both human and demonic leaders were intimidated—all powers felt the displacement caused by the anointing upon His life. The atmosphere would suddenly change, and storms would suddenly brew. His authority over every kind of sickness, disease, and demon would manifest. None of His influence was the product of well-oiled public relations machinery, television, books, a large church, or any other natural element. It was all spiritual empowerment.

All of these apostolic proofs were also evident in His twelve followers, who, once the Spirit fell on them, evoked the same kind of response wherever they went. They had apostolic anointing that engendered signs and wonders of every type, always confronting mountaintop principalities. They were therefore subject to much suffering and persecution—further evidence of a fully functioning apostle.

Before we can fully displace powers and principalities, apostles will have to be properly positioned on the tops of the mountains. Again, an apostle is someone who has been given authority to displace top-of-the-mountain demons and bring the reign of heaven in their place. We will not fully take the mountain of government without this gift in place. The apostle gift is specifically a government gift, whether inside or outside of the church. This does not mean we will need the title of apostle, but only the actual anointing of apostle. I'm fairly convinced that modern-day apostles will function better with other titles than "apostle." It's a very distracting title and carries a great deal of baggage, particularly at this time. In fact, we could probably weed out 90 percent of so-called apostles just by informing them they can't use their title anymore. The love of the title is perhaps the *first* evidence of not really being one. The natural instinct of anyone who knows the responsibility associated with the call would be to run in the opposite direction.

It will take true prophets and wise men to uncover true apostles. Whether or not the title comes into play, God is now preparing and raising up apostles to possess the mountain of government. They will be humble, intimate servants of the Lord who carry great spiritual power and authority. They may either be the advisors (intercessors) of politicians or the politicians themselves. (These will be the natural disguises for an actual apostolic anointing. Many will be women, who are the key for the church being released into her full destiny.) Daniel, for example, had an apostolic anointing from a position of influence. Esther and Joseph had actual positions they operated from—as well as influence beyond the position. King David was a good example of a presidential/apostle type. He had the highest spiritual authority *and* natural authority in the land.

This apostolic positioning will increase more and more among the nations of the world as the mountain of the Lord's house is exalted above all others. One reason we haven't advanced as far as expected in this area is that Christians who have come into power in various national governments haven't always been apostolic Christians. By apostolic Christians, I mean that they have made it to the top of the mountain without carrying apostolic authority. Apart from apostolic anointing, there is no displacement authority. Therefore many of these Christians have fallen to the same corruption as their predecessors. Lucifer and his corrupting Girgashites have not been spiritually displaced by the angels that would normally accompany a true apostle.

The goal is not just to have Christians in high places, but rather to have Christians who are *called* to be in high places step into that role. And wearing a Christian label on our sleeve isn't the point. We need to realize that stealth authority and influence are much preferred over overt authority and influence. A low profile diffuses resistance from the opposition. Political righteousness isn't determined by whether someone calls himself a Christian or not, anyway. That's established by whether the political values they are prepared to defend or establish are actually righteous. A Christian who espouses abortion rights or the validity of gay marriages, for example, is worthless as a Christian candidate. If candidates don't understand righteous politics, they aren't anointed for this mountain.

This will change as the Elijah Revolution is released upon the nations. Sons and daughters of the King who understand the call to take the seven mountains will rise to the mountaintops. More important than their confession of faith will be their understanding of kingdom issues. Do they understand God's redemptive plan for Israel in these last days? Do they understand that if you touch Israel, you touch the apple of His eye? (See Zechariah 2:8.) Entire nations will be severely judged or highly blessed and favored based on this issue alone. Governing cannot be done by the flesh anymore, as the issues will be increasingly highly charged spiritual matters that God will directly address—often through devastating judgments. (See Isaiah 26:9.)

The world will come to learn, for example, that though God passionately loves every homosexual, remaining in that sin will cause someone to fall under the sword of His judgment. Feelings don't validate a homosexual lifestyle any more than they validate a murderer's desire to kill. We are all born with feelings that we must curb and cut off, and the sooner we embrace God's standards, the sooner we have a chance to be at peace with Him. It is well understood that any child, when left to his or her own standards based on a feeling, will become a spoiled, unruly brat. What comes to us naturally is sin. We will lie, cheat, fornicate, dishonor our parents, and commit every other form of sin when we define righteousness by whatever we think we were born with. The sooner we understand that God expects righteousness—regardless of what our innate tendencies tell us—the sooner we will be able to eliminate His judgments from our personal and corporate lives.

One of the primary roles of future government leaders will be to instruct in righteousness. The more God's judgments are poured out on earth, the more explicitly will they be able to give that instruction.

THE LEVELS OF THE MOUNTAIN

As I covered in the first chapter, there are three levels of a mountain: the top, the middle, and the base. The top of the mountain is our objective; that's the nature of the tsunami's grace that is being released. That's where Lucifer is entrenched in some capacity or another, and that's where the stronghold of corruption is. "Top of the mountain" can apply at a national level or at a city or regional level. The promise is that nations are to be taken by the light on the sons and daughters of God.

The top of the mountain is held by a visible face, like the president, and the spiritual influence that has him there. We must always make a distinction between the natural faces and the ruling powers that influence them. We could become wrongly obsessed with changing only the physical people in power, not realizing that unless the mountain is simultaneously secured spiritually, a new person in office will likely succumb to the prevailing demonic influence over that area of the mountain. That's what has happened even in the U.S. Supreme Court, as Republican presidents have appointed apparent conservatives who then, inexplicably, begin to vote with the liberal block. They are conditioned by the not-yet-displaced powers over Washington, D.C. Ruling powers always affect the thought life of those under their geographical sphere. Judges may have a history of ruling one way in their home state, yet the spiritual climate of Washington, positioned under the influence of a larger demon, can cultivate another response from them.

Other levels of the mountain include lower political positions—anything from governors to judges to mayors. We need to fill the entire mountain with children of the kingdom who know why they are there: to allow the Lord's house to be exalted. This mountain has many niches and grooves and many ways to approach it. Some may be called to go after unjust laws as their arena of action. Others may be called to formulate foreign policy or push for budget reform. The more significant the repercussions of those laws and policies, the higher the mountain level represented. However high we go, enough grace will be provided because this is our promised land.

WHAT THE BIBLE SAYS ABOUT GOVERNMENT

I've already addressed many scriptures about the call to take nations that would also be applicable here, but here are some others:

> When the righteous are in authority, the people rejoice; But when a wicked man rules, the people groan.
>
> —PROVERBS 29:2

This is a good verse for those who doubt whether God would even want us involved in civil affairs. This is why the mountain of the Lord's house will be exalted. The peoples of the world are exhausted and "groaning" under the rule of wicked people. Every form of government has been tried, and all have failed dramatically. There is no new government prototype to try, and the earth knows it. It's groaning and travailing for those who keep their promises of righteousness and justice. Most politicians pledge to fight corruption, but few have been successful. All promise justice, but none are able to bring it about. The world's thinking is disconnected, as few seem to realize that only the influence of the Kingdom of God can bring about a real change. Only *He* is the desire of the nations (Haggai 2:7).

> For unto us a Child is born, Unto us a Son is given; And the government will be upon His shoulder, and His name will be called Wonderful, Counselor, Mighty God, Everlasting Father, Prince of Peace. Of the increase of His government and peace There will be no end, Upon the throne of David and over His kingdom, To order it and establish it with judgment and justice From that time forward and even forever. The zeal of the Lord of hosts will perform this.
>
> —ISAIAH 9:6–7

This powerful passage is a prophetic announcement of the coming of Jesus. Though we have secured elements of truth from this scripture, we have missed the eschatology it lays out. This Jesus who is coming will carry "government" on His shoulder (literally "back"); His rule and reign are being released through His coming. It is the

Lord Jesus who will show up, not just the *Savior* Jesus. He is coming to Earth with heaven's government on His back—and of the increase of His government there will be no end!

Jesus has no intention of visiting temporarily to see who wants to get saved. He will release His government and rule upon the earth—through His sons and daughters—and His kingdom will never stop growing. He *never* gives the planet to Satan! The takeover of the affairs of Earth is somehow tied into bringing order to the entire universe. Our planet is the last bastion of rebellion, and He will overwhelm it on His terms *here on this planet*. His terms? That His weak, foolish, simple, love-struck sons and daughters finally wake up to their inheritance and become the instruments that crush Satan—here and now.

This awakening will be so profound in His church that even the gates of hell will not prevail against it. (See Matthew 16:18.) Gates, of course, are defensive. Jesus will have a generation that will take all the land assigned to it and push Satan out of the second heaven—at the top of the mountains—all the way back into hell where he belongs. Apparently, he'll experience the surprise of our ability even to chase him into hell as his gates collapse. I, for one, intend to demand some personal payback from him and his minions at that time with whatever leeway that authority gives us.

THE DIFFERENCE BETWEEN CIVIL AND SPIRITUAL AUTHORITY

An area of confusion needs to be addressed here, as it is already causing turmoil in countries where the mountain of government is being taken by sons and daughters of the kingdom. The confusion arises in misunderstanding the difference between civil authority and spiritual authority. When a person known for spiritual authority steps into a position of civil authority, people wrongly transfer their expectations from one area to the other.

Spiritual authority comes from one's standing before God and refers to influence in heavenly places. It could also be considered as one's position of influence among believers. Civil authority is also a God-given authority, but it's very different. Someone may be granted civil authority by the Lord yet still be headed for hell. Civil authority governs society, while spiritual authority governs the church and the spirit realm. Many understand this concept pretty well until someone established as a spiritual authority comes into a position of civil authority and must then exercise authority differently.

I recently saw a perfect example of this. In a South American country, a pastor friend of mine entered politics very late in life. As leader of a large church, he had a well-established ministry and great spiritual authority among believers and was well respected throughout the nation. When led by the Lord to cross over into politics, he was suddenly thrust into the national spotlight. He resigned from his church to fill a prestigious political position, where he is now helping set the political agenda for the nation.

During election season, he was asked if he thought the death penalty should be invoked for a certain heinous crime. My friend said that he would in fact support the death penalty for this crime. That caused a bit of an uproar, both in secular circles as well as among Christians. How could a pastor be *for* the death penalty? many asked. This line of questioning arose because of confusion regarding the two types of authority. The expectation was that my friend would continue to represent himself as a spiritual authority when the issue at hand was of civil authority. Neither the world nor the church knew what to do with a pastor who supported putting someone to death.

I had an opportunity to speak into the situation, and I used Romans 13:1–4 as a foundation for understanding the matter:

> Let every soul be subject to the governing authorities. For there is no authority except from God, and the authorities that exist are appointed by God. Therefore whoever resists the authority resists the ordinance of God, and those who resist will bring judgment on themselves. For rulers are not a terror to good works, but to evil. Do you want to be unafraid of the authority? Do what is good, and you will have praise from the same. For he is God's minister to you for good. But if you do evil, be afraid; for he does not bear the sword in vain; for he is God's minister, an avenger to execute wrath on him who practices evil.
>
> —ROMANS 13:1–4

This is such a key area that we not only need to personally understand it, but also to be able to explain it to secular society. When a minister of the gospel of Jesus Christ accepts a civil role, he must fulfill the God-ordained responsibility assigned to a civil authority. Both spiritual and civil authority are ordained by God, but wielding that authority looks very different for each. One's role as a spiritual authority is to lead by example and not by constraint. (See 1 Peter 5:2.) It is a grace-based position of leadership and trust, and at no time is a spiritual authority to use his position to terminate someone's life. That position never requires force or intimidation—except when it opposes spiritual forces of iniquity.

A civil ruler, on the other hand, is entrusted with an entirely different authority. A central purpose of a civil ruler's call is to deal with lawlessness. Striking terror in the hearts of evildoers fulfills a specific assignment for which he will be accountable to God. Note that according to the scripture passage above, "he does not bear the sword in vain" and he is "God's minister" while doing this. Obviously, the sword was not for shaving. It was an instrument of death. Those in a position of civil authority must be prepared to fulfill the God-given demands of that role. Those who cannot do that must remain in the spiritual arena of authority. This is an important distinction.

My pastor/politician friend carries both types of authority and needs only to make it clear which authority he is speaking from. He is in favor of the death penalty in extreme cases, but he himself would not want to be the one to perform the execution because of his recognized spiritual authority. Though regularly interviewed because of his standing as a spiritual leader in the nation, he has to be willing to declare himself in favor of severe punishment for evildoers. Otherwise, the country would be afraid to make him president. No one wants a civil leader who is not willing to forcefully resist those who would harm or even invade the country.

As I write this, President George W. Bush is a Christian who also serves as civil leader of the most powerful nation on Earth. This position carries great responsibility—beyond what most people understand. "Most powerful nation" status is given by God; just as He places leaders *in* nations, He also establishes leadership *among* nations. President Bush reportedly relies on his personal walk with the Lord for guidance. But it's important to know that he has a biblical, God-ordained command to exercise "the sword" to stop those who would do evil. Confronting evil and delivering practical justice is a central call of those in civil positions of authority.

A new model of national leadership will develop as God exalts His mountain above all other mountains. There will be Joseph-type presidents of nations who will carry great spiritual authority and great civil authority. At various times, these presidents will need to step back and forth between those roles and address the concerns of each. There will be times to address the nation and say, "I will now speak to you outside of my civil authority but in my capacity as a minister and servant of God." One can then address the moral and righteousness issues of the nation and speak out of the spiritual authority God has given him or her.

It needs to be addressed here because understanding this dynamic will be so crucial as the Lord raises us up to lead our countries. We cannot exert the same type of authority over a nation that we exert over a church. As civil leaders who have been called to lead churches have to adjust from the civil authority model to a more benevolent spiritual leadership, so will church leaders who have been called into government need to adjust their use of authority. We must understand the interplay and the limits on civil and spiritual leadership models.

THE MULTI-PRONGED APPROACH TO TAKING THE MOUNTAIN

The mountain of government is so expansive that it would be impossible to lay forth all the strategies that the Lord might reveal for targeting the top of it. He could have us get behind existing or emerging righteous politicians, form new political parties for Him to raise up through His tsunami of grace, fund efforts to implement legal changes, and seek out and support those who carry an apostolic grace for this mountain. He will reveal strategies for local, state, and national politics, and they could be endless. Regardless of the specific strategy, the main thing is to do it from one's position as a son or daughter of the kingdom. This is a spiritual ministry and a kingdom of God venture.

We must approach this mountain as those whose citizenship is in heaven. (See Philippians 3:20.) In the latter days, the Lord will use citizens of heaven who live on Earth to exalt the His mountain above all other mountains. This citizenship must transcend our natural citizenship. Our natural citizenship is still important, as it establishes a specific arena where we're called to be active. But it's as citizens of heaven that we are sold out to our King and consumed by a deep love for Him, positioning ourselves to receive empowered strategy from heaven to fast forward His prayer while He was on earth: "Your Kingdom come. Your will be done On earth as it is in heaven" (Matt. 6:10).

BEWARE OF STRATEGIES OF THE FLESH

It's important at this point to warn of strategies of the flesh that are sourced by human, carnal thinking. The natural mind is at enmity with God and cannot be the source for a God idea. (See Romans 8:7.)

> No one knows the things of God except the Spirit of God. Now we have received, not the spirit of the world, but the Spirit who is from God, that we might know the things that have been freely given to us by God. These things we also speak, not in words which man's wisdom teaches but which the Holy Spirit teaches, comparing spiritual things with spiritual. But the natural man does not receive the things of the Spirit of God, for they are foolishness to him; nor can he know them, because they are spiritually discerned...But we have the mind of Christ.
>
> —1 CORINTHIANS 2:11–16

Strategies of the flesh are possibly the greatest snare we will face in taking the mountains of our nations. Almost every move of God is preceded by a false start through human-originated tactics. This is true of much of what we see as "apostolic" today. A fleshly strategy comes out of locking onto a revelation or promise of God and attempting to pull it off with a worldly approach. It's usually highly logical and appeals to the natural man, but it carries no accompanying power of God—and will, in fact, finally war against that which is coming in the Spirit.

A perfect example of this is the story of Abraham and the promise of Isaac. Abraham was a godly man who was given a promise of a son named Isaac. When the God-given strategy—bearing this child through his wife Sarah in their old age—seemed to delay, he resorted to a strategy of the flesh. He attempted to bring forth the godly promise through Hagar, Sarah's handmaiden. All that produced was Ishmael, who would then become Isaac's greatest in-house antagonist.

How to Determine Your Strategy

How do you judge the source of a strategy? It often requires years of hearing and obeying God to learn to discern the difference between what is of the flesh and what came from the Spirit. In order to receive a God-strategy, one must start from a foundation of emptiness before the Lord. This must be followed by a period of inquiring of the Lord, and there are no time limits on this period. God may respond immediately or delay. A delay means that God must first strip you of all confidence in the flesh that would potentially be a snare.

A God-given strategy for anything will always carry some element of the impossible in it. If your strategy is entirely possible, it is not God's strategy. You could do it without Him. God's strategy will always require the activation of faith because without faith, it is impossible to please God. (See Hebrews 11:6.) It is also impossible to access the supernatural realm without faith. Faith is essential for taking this mountain of government and every other mountain. As we have seen, Abraham's faith test was that a woman with a dead womb would bring forth a child. Logic (the natural mind) told him that the woman with a living womb had to be the source—the Hagar solution. God could not honor that which proceeded from the wisdom of man.

The Prayer Strategy

A strategy that God has already revealed for everything in life is that we must begin and finish in prayer. We must constantly acknowledge, "I'm really powerless, too weak to pull this off." Even Jesus—God in the flesh—when reduced to human restrictions, could not advance without continuous prayer. He constantly pulled aside for prayer, and before His final test on the cross He was in prevailing, travailing prayer in Gethsemane.

Scripture is also clear on the priority of praying for political leaders.

> Therefore I exhort first of all that supplications, prayers, intercessions, and giving of thanks be made for all men, for kings and all who are in authority.
>
> —1 TIMOTHY 2:1–2

This passage establishes a "first of all" priority of praying for those in authority. It is particularly insightful when we realize that Nero, one of the Roman Empire's most evil, treacherous emperors, was the ruler in authority when Paul wrote this.

Many nations are in different stages of advancement in God's end-time plan. Remember that it's in the latter days when He begins to take over nations through His citizens of heaven who live on Earth. It all starts with a heavy prayer canopy over the kings or presidents in office. Remarkably, we're told to give thanks even for undesirables—remember, Paul was writing under the reign of a Christian-killing emperor. So our prayer cover over a nation's key leadership post is to begin with gratitude for a silver lining, even in the worst of governments. As we establish a prayer canopy over the office itself, heaven's help is released into the matter. Our prayers of covering begin to neutralize hell's access to that office.

We see this played out in the book of Esther, where an evil king (as history describes him) is moved to make righteous decrees through the intercession of a righteous woman (Esther). It isn't always necessary to wait for a Christian to be in office in order for that office to release righteous judgments. Committed prayer warriors can impose heaven's will and cause the precious to be extracted from the worthless. (See Jeremiah 15:9.) No matter how grievous or difficult the task of taking a nation's mountain of government may be, prayer is the most powerful ingredient of any possible strategy. It must dislodge and displace. The action steps are to ensure that no vacuum is left in the wake of a dislodged government.

THE ACTION STRATEGY

Prayer strategies must be accompanied or soon followed by actual action steps. As James said, "Faith without works is dead" (James 2:14–26). At some point, faith has to be demonstrated by action. For us, that means that we can't only have a prayer strategy for defeating Lucifer, his Girgashites, and his human pawns. We must also work to raise up that which will keep the enemy displaced.

If Washington, D.C., is the geographical top of the mountain, then at some point we must embark on a holy invasion of that stronghold. We see this already taking place with new ministries coming and physically spending a lot of time in the D.C. area. Prayer warriors, as well as those called to be the new visible faces on this mountain, need to invade.

If Harvard is a seedbed for the future leaders who will occupy the top of the mountain of politics, then it needs to be a part of the multi-pronged strategy. We need a host of Elijah revolutionaries to go and attend that school and bring the order of heaven to that place—a strategy we'll discuss in much greater detail in the next chapter. Christians at Harvard is not a new concept, but Elijah revolutionaries on that campus would be. An Elijah revolutionary lives out of his kingdom identity. He or she is first and foremost a citizen of heaven, and only secondarily is he a citizen of his nation. A revolutionary will carry the zeal of the Lord for righteousness and justice—which are the foundations of His throne. (See Psalm 97:2.) Harvard will again burn with transformational governmental righteousness that will bring light to the nations of the world. As I'm writing, I'm prophetically seeing these things for Harvard and how that is a key part of the action strategy for taking the land that the Lord has given us at the top of the mountain of government.

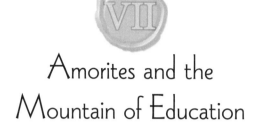

Amorites and the
Mountain of Education

A T THE END of the last chapter, we discussed the role of Harvard and its impact on government. Harvard is at a very significant intersection between that mountain and the mountain of education. There are others, of course, as all of these mountains are interrelated to some degree. Each one influences the others. It's easy to think that taking just the media mountain, for example, would take care of the rest of them, and that rings true, to a point. We could also say that taking the government mountain gives us the others. Each one of these mountains carries huge sway toward winning the hearts and minds of humanity. As we delve into this mountain of education, we will see how important and influential it is.

WHAT IS EDUCATION?

Education is knowledge or a skill obtained or developed by a learning process. In many ways in the West, it has been hijacked from its original objectives. This mountain has been infiltrated and taken over by forces opposed to those originally intended to be there. Most American educational institutions, for example, were meant to serve as places of training and admonition in the fear of God. Their instruction was given in the context of a worldview that put God in the center of life as the One around whom we all must orbit. God was the foundation of all areas of learning.

America's first public school was established in 1635 by noted Puritan minister John Cotton. Virtually all early public schools had ministers as headmasters. Reading, writing, and arithmetic were always of secondary value compared to instruction in the ways of

God. In order to prepare for life in this world, students needed to know how to relate to God and how to orbit around who He is and what He expects.

Harvard, William and Mary, Yale, and Princeton are the four oldest learning institutions in the United States. Each has produced noted presidents and leaders. And all four have strayed far from their roots. They need to be brought back into their original destiny.

Harvard University was formed in 1636. The principal donor for its foundation was a clergyman named John Harvard, from whom the university derives its name. It is the oldest learning institution in America and was established for the purpose of training and releasing into society clergymen and scholars with Puritan values. Its motto is *Veritas,* which means "truth." It presently has the largest endowment of any university in the world—$27.6 billion. Seven American presidents, including George W. Bush, have attended Harvard. It is arguably the most prestigious educational institution in the world.

William and Mary College was established in 1693 and is the second oldest learning institution in America. It was originally founded as an Anglican school. Its governors were required to be members of the Church of England and to agree to adhere to its thirty-nine articles. Three former U.S. presidents were educated there.

Yale University was founded in 1701 by ten congregational ministers and is the country's third oldest learning institution. Its endowment is second only to Harvard. Jonathan Edwards, the great theologian, revivalist, and leader of the Great Awakening, attended Yale—the divinity school houses a Jonathan Edwards Center devoted to the study of his works. Five U.S. presidents attended Yale. (George W. Bush, an undergraduate at Yale and a graduate of Harvard Business School, is claimed by both universities.)

Princeton University was formed in 1746 and is the fourth oldest learning institution of America. Its motto is Under God's Power She Flourishes. Princeton was established by Presbyterians and was designed to train Presbyterian ministers. Jonathan Edwards was briefly the president of Princeton in 1758, right before he died from a smallpox inoculation. Four U.S. presidents have come through Princeton.

These four universities alone are responsible for eighteen American presidents as well as many, many other national leaders around the world. They are clearly somewhere on the top of the mountain of education. Though they should be a beachhead for kingdom influence globally, they are instead a bastion for liberalism, which is manifested in a philosophy that displaces God from the center and puts man there instead.

A *Washington Post* article reported that 72 percent of the teachers in our institutions of higher learning are self-described liberals and 15 percent conservatives.[1] Again, conservatism doesn't equate to the kingdom of God, but they do espouse similar family values.

When you narrow the statistics only to those elite schools mentioned above, the imbalance is even worse. In these schools, liberal teachers—again, these are self-described—account for 87 percent of the total! We are, in essence, releasing our young people into humanistic (often atheistic) indoctrination by letting them attend the country's oldest and most respected universities. Unfortunately, even most of our Christian universities and colleges espouse something less than a kingdom perspective. Our seminaries often are even more toxic than the liberal institutions because students enter with the assumption that they will be learning more of the ways of God—but find a humanistic approach to the Bible.

Who Rules Education?

The third great enemy nation in Israel's Promised Land was the Amorites. (See Deuteronomy 7:1.) The word *Amorite* means "to boast," "to jut out," "mountaineer," "to act proudly," "pride in one's heart." Together these definitions describe the basic thought of humanism. The Amorites must be defeated in order to take the mountain of education.

Humanism is an ethical philosophy that prioritizes universal human qualities and intellect. It is empowered by rationalism. Humanism rejects the validity of transcendental justifications, such as dependence on faith, the supernatural, or divinely revealed truths. Greek philosophy and philosophers are the intellectual source of this way of thinking, but it came to dominate Western societies in the Enlightenment of the eighteenth century, which emphasized human reason as the only legitimate source of knowledge. Demonic principalities and powers are, of course, the "spiritual wickedness in high places" behind these *-isms*.

The Siamese twin of humanism is atheism—the belief that there is no God. Soon we will no longer have to deal with this. God's judgments will be so clearly manifested that there will be no doubt that there is a God. The only question will be, What are you going to do about it—bow or be destroyed? It really will be that simple.

Mainstream liberalism is the political cover for both humanism and atheism. (I'm aware that liberalism means different things to different people; in some countries it's actually the more conservative perspective. I'm using it here in the context of American political ideology.) I see liberalism as the cover for these philosophies because in liberalism one can theoretically believe in God without having to accept any of His standards (sanctity of life, sex only within heterosexual marriage, etc.) Liberalism keeps introducing new and improved versions of God, whose moral standards seem to fit the preferences of liberal society. If their perspective is accurate, He no longer values the institution of marriage that He created. Instead, He validates whatever we feel like doing. (Interestingly, the motto of the Satanic Bible is Do As Thou Wilt.) This god of liberalism did not necessarily create the world, yet he exists in some esoteric fashion.

Humanism engenders much philosophical hypocrisy. The same people who espouse total sexual freedom in the choice of partners and genders are also the most vocal voices of shock and outrage at the number of child sex slaves and AIDS orphans in the world. They are living in denial of the fact that the so-called freedoms they espouse are a primary cause of the very things they are outraged about. Once you cease to orbit around the Creator, you are truly lost. In humanism, God is meant to orbit around man—if He even exists at all.

The King of the Amorites

The Amorites on the mountain of education are humanism and its spin-offs of atheism, liberalism, and rationalism. These *-isms* are all lies that are being sold by a certain principality who sits at the top of the mountain and commands his Amorite army. This principality, I believe, is Beelzebub. His name means "Lord of the flies"—with flies representing the lies he tells. He's Baal of the lies. He is apparently a chief lieutenant of Lucifer, though he could be just another face of Satan—or Satan himself. Regardless of his exact identity, his denotation as Beelzebub gives us insight into his tool of advance, his lies. All effective lies carry a significant portion of truth. For the mouse, it's the cheese that carries the poison that kills him. Beelzebub has laid out mouse traps throughout the various spheres of education. We don't need to itemize the mouse traps of philosophy—that would be an endless, tedious task that many have been working at for years. God is about to spring all of these traps as He establishes the central truth that will soon resonate throughout the world. God's truths that counteract Beelzebub's lies are:

- There is a God.
- He is active in the affairs of men.
- He has definite standards of moral conduct.
- You must chose to embrace Him or you'll feel His wrath.

God's judgments are released specifically to counter and neutralize the deceptions of Satan. The coming judgments will be so targeted to the sin condition of a certain area, city, region, or nation that questions of *Was it God or not?* will eventually cease. Those who die in their sin will be those who never saw the connection. There are reasons New Orleans was vulnerable and could be so again. There's a reason that San Francisco is very vulnerable. Certain nations are vulnerable to profound judgments, and these judgments will be a major mark of the latter days.

Judgment will work with the spiritual tsunamis of God to bring revolutionary changes to cities and nations. God has pleaded with nations through His church and through the preaching of the gospel. He will now plead with the nations through His righteous judgments. Initially, His judgments will be acts of grace—pleas for repentance. His final judgments will be devastating, as they will come upon those

THE SEVEN MOUNTAIN PROPHECY

who, knowing He is God and knowing what He is looking for, still hardened their hearts.

There will be a direct connection between the mountain of education being taken and God's judgments being made manifest. Isaiah 26:9–10 specifically speaks of the inhabitants of the world having to learn righteousness. When the righteous rule on this mountain, the first line of learning they will release will be instruction in righteousness. The fear of the Lord is the beginning of wisdom, and wisdom is the goal of education. There can be no true wisdom that does not begin with a proper fear of the Lord. That fear will burn up Beelzebub's lies. If Beelzebub is the prince of Greece mentioned in Daniel 10:20—or a collaborator with that prince—education will be profoundly affected because this prince of Greece is the stronghold behind the mind of reason and rationalism.

THE IMPORTANT ROLE OF TEACHERS

On the first two mountains of media and government, I mentioned the key role of the biblical gifts of evangelists and apostles. In securing the mountain of education, the gift of teaching is very important. These must be Holy Spirit-empowered teachers, as opposed to secularly confirmed teachers. The biblical role of a teacher is to instruct in the ways of the Lord. The gifting empowers teachers to break down the lies of the enemy that come to this mountain. As the church, we are in much greater need of having these teachers in the education system than we are of having them in church. And having spiritually gifted teachers throughout the system isn't enough; the certification system and the curriculum itself must be overhauled.

FROM LEFT-BRAINISM TO RIGHT-BRAINISM

All Satan has to do is get us to buy into one philosophical lie, and he can then take captive an entire mountain. Right now, through Beelzebub and the Amorites, he has us living and experiencing education through a left-brain grid.

We are born with a right-brain processor and a left-brain processor.

That means that the left and right sides of our brain literally process information in an entirely different manner.

Our left brain is verbal and processes information analytically and sequentially. It looks first at the individual bites of information and then puts things together to get the whole. A left brain processes thoughts step by step. Words are the primary reminder of information. This side of our brain is highly organized and likes lists, planning, rules, and keeping time. It enjoys observing. It is logical, sequential, rational, analytical, and objective. The left brain listens to *what* is being said and communicates verbally.

Our right brain, however, is visual and processes information intuitively and simultaneously. It looks first at the whole picture and then examines the details. The right cerebral cortex is connected to the left cerebral cortex by masses of nerve fibers, which allow messages to pass between them. The right brain is the creative processor, while the left brain is robotic in accessing whatever is fed into it. Unlike the methodical approach of the left brain, the right brain processes all at once. Pictures (in the mind) are the key memories. The right brain is not highly organized but is organic in that it responds by free association. It likes to know the *why* of things. It is not sensitive to the issue of time. It enjoys participating—touching and feeling. It loves patterns, metaphors, analogies, role-playing, and visuals, and can be subjective and random. The right brain listens to *how* something is said, aiding our vocal inflection and mannerisms.

	Left Brain	**Right Brain**
Language	Words	Pictures
Processing	Analytical	Intuitive
Concept of Time	Sequential	Simultaneous
Favorite Questions	What?	Why? and How?
Mode of Learning	Observing	Participating
Perspective	Objective	Subjective
Expression	Logical	Creative

Upon entering school, most children are predominantly right-brain processors and thinkers.[2] It doesn't take long in our education system, however, for that to change dramatically. After just a couple of years of formal education, more than 90 percent of children are left-brain dominant. By the time they graduate from high school, more than 98 percent of kids are firmly left-brain dominant. The further they go in higher education, the more left-brain they become. Once all the masters and doctorates are included, hardly a blip remains of right-brain thinkers.

Most IQ and scholastic aptitude tests measure left-brain skills. Verbal skills, abstract thinking, mathematics, and inferential logic are all left-brain operations. Our educational system determines students' intelligence almost entirely by the proficiency of their left brain. Our educational system is toxic to the right-brain processor, causing us to switch from our natural right-brainism to left-brainism.

Most of us will, at different times, be able to identify varying pulls from both sides of our brains. They each have a voice. The problem is that when one side of the brain is stimulated and conditioned to be dominant, it invariably strong-arms the weaker side into submission. For many people, the right brain primarily serves as the nagging voice we never listen to.

Traditionally, women in particular are wired in such as way that they can have a difficult time squelching the right brain's input. She will have a feeling about someone, and it will drive a left-brain dominant man crazy. He considers such intuition as inferior brainpower, when it is actually the perfectly natural function of the other half of the brain. Many women are, therefore, more relationally gifted because they cannot ignore their right brain, no matter how much an educational system tries to weed it out of them. Though the educational system may have worked on her to suppress confidence in her intuition, she will, more likely than not, yield to it in relational matters. In suppressing the right brain, a goal of the demonic principality has also been to suppress women by demeaning their mental capabilities.

WHAT IS KINGDOM THINKING?

So what's wrong with being left-brain dominant? If you don't understand all the extended implications of how you are trained to think, you may not see what the problem is. Let's take a look at Scripture's emphasis for some insights.

Jesus came into a very left-brain culture. It was totally dominated by Greek thought. In other words, rationalism prevailed. Even the right-brain Hebraic culture had been influenced by its sweeping dominance. Into this setting stepped God in the flesh. His ministry was first announced by John the Baptist:

> In those days John the Baptist came preaching in the wilderness of Judea, and saying, "Repent, for the kingdom of heaven is at hand!"
>
> —MATTHEW 3:1–2

Jesus Himself then spoke as He started His ministry in the next chapter:

> From that time Jesus began to preach and to say, "Repent for the kingdom of heaven is at hand!"
>
> —MATTHEW 4:17

These passages are saying a little bit more than most of us have realized. John the Baptist first comes and essentially says, "Repent. You are about to see the rule and reign of heaven manifested." Then Jesus comes and uses that same word—*repent*. We have always understood that to mean "be sorry for your sins." The original Greek word, however, is a much more profound instruction. *Metanoeo* literally means "to change one's mind, to think differently, to do an 'about face' in one's thinking." It's all about how one thinks. John and Jesus were addressing, at least in part, the prevailing Greek thinking of the day. John prepared the way of the Lord by saying, "Hey, guys and gals, a man sent from heaven is about to show up, and He's going to blow your mind with what He's going to say and do. If you stay in your 'left processor,' you are not going to understand Him because He is going to violate everything your processor has ever learned."

Jesus then showed up, said the same thing, and began to demonstrate what He was talking about. It was as if He was saying, "You'd better let your right brain function, or else you're going to resist me and miss out on what I have to show you from the realm of heaven. I'm going to manifest the King's dominion to you, and your Greek thought is going to get trashed. You've been taught that one plus one is two, and two plus two is four. I'll show you that one can put a thousand to flight and two can chase ten thousand. I'll show how two fish and five pieces of bread can feed more than five thousand. And to really mess with your left brain, there will be more left over than there was to start with! I'm going to cause a blind man to see by spitting in dirt and rubbing mud in his eye. I'm going to heal a paralytic by telling him his sins are forgiven. I'm going to heal many others by telling them I sense their faith. I'm going to speak to storms—did they teach you that in school?—and they will obey me. I'm going to defy laws of physics and walk on water.

"In the midst of all this, I'll teach you the philosophical opposite of what you've been instructed. I'll tell you that if you want to be great, you must become nothing. If you want to live, you must die. If you want to go up, you must go down. If you want to learn how to win friends and influence people, you'd better take your eyes off of friends and people and find out what influences the invisible realm. I'll then choose and train twelve backward, volatile fishermen and use them as the antithesis of what you've been taught to value. Then I'll make my kingly entrance into Jerusalem on the back of a donkey, just to make sure your left processor really blows a gasket. In my closing act, I'll claim my lordship over this world by allowing Myself to be brutally beaten, spit at, and humiliated so that through My death, you all can live. You'd better *metanoeo* now, or you just won't get it—or get Me or the benefits of the very God who created you. Your natural mind the way it presently operates is at total odds with Me and what I bring."

It's important that we be confronted with certain realities about left- and right-brain thinking. Left-brain thinking, when it becomes dominant, squeezes out the things of the Spirit of God. The right brain isn't the kingdom of God, but it's the part of the brain God has created to be open to respond to His ways. It's the chimney through which faith is accessed. You can't do that with the left brain. You can quote all the scriptures on faith and understand the logic of faith, but only the right brain can tap into the actual substance of faith. That, of course, is a huge deal, since scripture tells us that "without faith it is impossible to please God" (Hebrews 11:6) and that "whatever is not from faith is sin" (Rom. 14:23). All the fruit of the Spirit—love, joy, peace, etc.—are all accessed only through the right brain. The left brain can understand the logic of peace, for example, but only the right brain can obtain and experience the peace that passes understanding.

Nearly everything Jesus did or said pulled on the right brain. His principles were upside-down from Greek thought. His power baffled Greek computations. The way He randomly switched His power techniques was confusing. He did no two recorded miracles the same way. He usually spoke in parables—word pictures that appeal to the right brain. He often said things that frustrate left-brain-oriented people— "The kingdom of God is like a treasure hidden in a field," for example (Matt. 13:44). In fact, *all* of His descriptions of the kingdom of God were pictures, stories, or metaphors.

Jesus certainly wasn't anti-intellectual, but He was clearly anti-left-brain intellect. Made in His image, we are wired to respond to the logic of heaven. We yearn for the supernatural, for the invisible, for the impossible to become possible—for the kingdom of God. We have been blinded to our true heart's desires by being indoctrinated in skepticism, doubt, and unbelief—our condition when the left-brain becomes dominant.

The left brain is designed to serve the interests of the right brain. It is supposed to help us organize and keep time while we access reality with the right brain. Instead of submitting the right brain to left-brain rationalism, we were created to submit the left brain to right brain perceptions.

DEVELOPING NEW CURRICULUM

This problem of left-brain domination has affected us in more ways than we can imagine. It is one of the ultimate strongholds in many arenas of life that has caused the church to see much less of God and His power. Left-brain thinking shapes all of our educational institutions, even our seminaries. It determines the careers we value—compare the pay scales for lawyers, doctors, and bankers to those of artists, musicians, and writers, for example—as well as the kind of man we want our daughters to marry. (How many parents encourage their daughters to find a good poet?) The rewards of society generally go to the most left-brained among us. The exceptions, of course, are the less than 1 percent of the entertainers, athletes, and artists who make it big. But relatively speaking, they are rare. This design is manipulated by principalities and powers.

So the assignment for Holy Spirit-gifted teachers is much more profound than it appears at first glance. We don't just need teachers out there in the world to be an available Christian influence. We don't need people who will just stand for creationism and the Ten Commandments. The whole system is wired wrongly through its obsession with left-brain curriculum. Creationism may seem unbelievable when you live out of your left brain and are not accessing things of the Spirit of God through the right brain. The left brain is conditioned by Beelzebub/the prince of Greece to reject a Creator God. Left-brain dominance rules out supernatural answers to anything. It has a theoretical grid for the supernatural but no practical grid by which to understand it. Ironically, it takes a greater leap of faith to believe in a big bang theory not tied into God.

God is going to raise up a new breed of Elijah Revolution teachers to invade the mountain of education. On-fire, passionate, Holy Spirit-filled teachers who are gifted and empowered will give education an extreme makeover. Having Christian teachers who are logical, analytical, and inexperienced in the things of the Spirit won't help us very much. We need teachers either to get a baptism in fire or be replaced by those who better represent the kingdom of God. These new education revolutionaries will develop new curricula that will be attractive and insightful even to the secular world, which is even now beginning to admit that the present system stifles creativity.

A sweeping new educational system that reflects a switch from left- to right-brain thinking will come into view. It will be enthusiastically embraced because kids will enjoy it much more than the left-brain model—and because calling out the creative side of children will surface genius giftings in many of them. Kids' appetite for the supernatural is already insatiable, as evidenced by the way they flock to movies, video games, books, magazines, and TV shows with supernatural themes. It's the way God has wired this generation; He's prepared them to expect and receive the miraculous. The church can either provide the real thing in its proper context or continue to let the media and the occult feed them the counterfeits. If we won't prophesy, they'll turn to psychic networks. If we won't heal, they'll seek out witch doctors with miracle cures. If we don't lead them into the presence of God, they'll find something else—New Age, drugs, music, Harry Potter, or anything else—to stimulate their otherwise lifeless heart. One way or another, this generation will escape the left-brain deadness of our culture. The way God has preconditioned this generation makes it ripe and ready for an extreme makeover. The opportunity to topple this left-brain, human-reason-exalting, already-wobbling mountain has opened up for us. *But* we have to be prepared to exalt the Lord's mountain in its place.

The Levels of the Mountain

As always, my description of the mountain's levels is not meant to be scientific—which shouldn't cause you any concern if you're beginning to function a little more out of your right brain.

The top of this mountain, as with the others, influences millions and is the part we have specifically been given grace to target. The tsunami will help us get up there by raising us to higher ground. We will displace Beelzebub and his humanistic Amorites, and we'll establish a foundation of God-centeredness on the peak. The natural institutions that now occupy the top are Harvard, Princeton, and Yale, with some others not far behind. It is not inconceivable that an extreme makeover of those three universities would impact many other schools of learning. Elijah revolutionaries can re-dig the original spiritual well from which these institutions sprang. They were established to reach the nations, to teach a righteous curriculum, to establish national policy on many fronts, and to raise godly leaders for the nations. They just aren't doing it very well right now because they are under the influence of Beelzebub and the Amorites, who dominate the mountain.

Lower down the mountain, we need to fill teaching positions with Elijah revolutionaries who can begin to initiate an extreme educational makeover. This mountain needs to be invaded by citizens of heaven who know who they are and what they are on the mountain to do.

WHAT THE BIBLE SAYS ABOUT EDUCATION

Train up a child in the way that he should go, And when he is old he will not depart from it.

—PROVERBS 22:6

The Hebrew word for "train up" is *chanak*, which means "to make narrow." An alternative meaning is "to strangle"—in this context, by choking out the lies. This verse establishes a couple of very important points. First, a child *does* have to be trained up in the way he should go. What he naturally feels is not valid simply because he feels it. There are influences and behavior that need to be "strangled" out through this training. The training is to put a child on a narrow path—the instruction of the Lord. Second, the training one receives as a child will guide him when he is older. That's why education is so important and why Satan has strategically invaded this mountain. He wants to capture subsequent generations. We can—and we will—take back this mountain. For the sake of future generations, we must.

A MULTI-PRONGED APPROACH

Because this mountain is so large, it must be approached in many, many ways. Intercessors need to invade by filling this mountain with their prayers. Prophets need to invade by speaking and releasing the future for this mountain. Apostles need to camp outside the spiritual walls of Harvard, Yale, and Princeton and offer prayers and worship until the walls crumble. The multi-pronged approach, as always, involves both the removal of something old and the establishment of something new. Spiritual forces have to be defeated and their pawns—whether people or institutions—must either be converted or removed.

If your heart burns for this mountain, seek God and find out which column you are to march in. This and all other mountains will be filled with the army of Elijah revolutionaries, as described by Joel:

> Their appearance is like the appearance of horses; And like swift steeds, so they run. With a noise like chariots Over mountains they leap, Like the noise of a flaming fire that devours the stubble, Like a strong people set in battle array. Before them the people writhe in pain; All faces are drained of color. They run like mighty men, They climb the wall like men of war; Every one marches in formation, and they do not break ranks. They do not push one another; Every one marches in his own column. Though they lunge between the weapons, They are not cut down. They run to and fro in the city, They run on the wall; They climb into the houses, They enter at the windows like a thief. The earth quakes before them... The LORD gives voice before His army, For His camp is very great.
>
> —JOEL 2:4–11

The opening line is insightful, as it relates specifically to this mountain of education. "Their appearance is like horses." Horses are often understood to represent truth. His truth marches on. They were made for running in, and even over, mountains. Horses stomp out flies (the lies of Beelzebub). Flies always pester horses, but just a twitch or a shake of the tail gets rid of them. Flies cannot compete for horses' terrain. They have no power compared to horses; a running, leaping horse doesn't even see a fly. As we start to run, the flies—the lies of the enemy—will flee, and God will release earthquakes ahead of us so tsunami waves can propel us to our promised land at the top of the mountain. This is not triumphalism, and it may not be easy. However, it is still our destiny. The enemy on this mountain must be put under Jesus' feet.

THE PRAYER STRATEGY

Some of our prayer strategy for this mountain has already been sprinkled throughout the previous pages of this chapter. The main point is to remember that this is a spiritual battle, so prayer must precede and accompany whatever strategy God gives. Prayer is the alpha and omega of the assignment because it directly accesses He who is the Alpha and Omega—He who starts and finishes a good work.

Prayers must be right-brain driven. The strategy may or may not be very logical to the left brain, but the right brain runs on a logic of its own. That logic is not a normal, rational, cause-and-effect strategy. The reasoning of the right brain is that if God said to do it, it will have powerful consequences. Marching around walls, for example, shouldn't cause them to collapse as it did at Jericho. Neither should blowing a shofar cause enemy forces to begin killing each other. Yet these and many other seemingly non-associated acts of obedience are the Bible's model for us. This does not compute with the left brain. But the greatest logic that exists is that obedience to God accesses the power of His kingdom. If we will *metanoeo,* He will begin to reveal secrets and mysteries that can fast-forward His work.

THE ACTION STRATEGY

As I've stated, targeting top-of-the-mountain institutions such as Harvard, Princeton, and Yale is central to this action strategy. We need intentional groups of Elijah revolutionaries to band together and penetrate into these schools by attending them as their mission from God. Little sparks in these schools will create great fires. There will be significant and revolutionary revivals in all of these institutions, and when they take place, they will need to bring about wholesale infrastructural changes. There will eventually be professors at these institutions who have read this very book and will become transformers for the kingdom of God, as they realize they were created for such a time as this.

The action strategy needs to be implemented at the student level, the faculty level, and curriculum level. Elijah revolutionaries can be either the direct movers and shakers or a supporter and influencer of them. Someone may already have the next anointed curriculum to invade the school system. Somebody else might have the finances to get that curriculum pushed forward. The nations themselves are ready for it.

"Jesus" doesn't have to be stamped all over a curriculum for it to be anointed and useful. It's possible to have one that leads horses to the water without forcing them to drink. The kingdom of God always advances under free will. He let one of His twelve disciples reject and betray Him. Taking over this mountain does not imply imposing religion on anyone. It simply creates a level playing field that allows the Christian belief in God to compete with all other religions. If we present the true gospel of Jesus, He will be so attractive that He will draw all men to Himself.

Canaanites and the
Mountain of Economy

THE MOUNTAIN OF economy could also be called the mountain of wealth or the mountain of money. Money and resources are discussed often in scripture, and with very good reason. We have a saying about deciphering the root of a shady situation: Just follow the money. Presidents and world leaders are usually elected and/or ejected over the issue of how they've handled the national economy. Virtually all corruption issues have to do with greed or poverty. Taking this mountain will require utmost care and caution, as the enemies on it are very deceitful.

An Internet definition of *economy* is "a system of production and distribution and consumption." Another definition is "the efficient use of resources." When applied at a national or big-picture level, the economy is the proper flow and balance of the production of resources, the distribution of resources, and the consumption of resources. An economy is healthy when there's a proper relationship between these three elements. The most common area of breakdown and corruption is between production and distribution.

The world economy functions under very complex and multifaceted influences, and world economists widely disagree among themselves on the cause and effect of all the different pieces of the economic puzzle. They not only disagree on the future outlook of world and various national economies; they also debate each other's interpretation of the reasons behind historical collapses and boons. I will share in layman's terms my understanding of world economics because it is important to understand in order to take this mountain. If I'm technically wrong on an issue of analysis, please pardon my inexperience in this area. Regardless of the finer details, however, I believe my conclusions are warranted.

Theoretically, world money traders create economic realities. More than a trillion dollars are traded every day just in world currency speculations.[1] These traders examine the latest external and internal reports on a nation's economic health and determine the value of that nation's currency. They buy currencies that seem to be strengthening and sell currencies that seem to be weakening. A significant sell-off of a currency can then create its own ripple effect, where traders get rid of a currency solely because others are getting rid of it. Rumors and perceptions are as powerful as realities in this world of high finances. Theoretically, this daily activity has more power to determine a nation's financial health than any real economic action taking place in that nation.

Case in point: the great Asian economic collapse of 1997 profoundly affected nations like Indonesia, South Korea, Thailand, and Malaysia. For various reasons, world currency traders lost confidence in these economies. It started with one, and then an amazing domino effect began to take place. No one knew when it was going to stop. Its ripples extended worldwide, and eventually Mexico and Brazil were adversely affected.

In hindsight, it seems that world currency speculators overreacted to certain reports and trends. In doing so, they threw several nations into a spiraling economic crisis. Indonesia's rupiah went from two thousand to eighteen thousand per U.S. dollar—a 900 percent devaluation. During that year, sixty million middle- to upper-middle-class Indonesians fell below the poverty line. No famine, earthquake, tsunami, or any other tangible event created this cause and effect. This devastation was arguably created by world currency speculators, as fears and concerns prompted them to overreact. Though some were accused of currency manipulation—conspiring to bring down these national economies—that doesn't appear to be even logistically possible. They simply responded out of their own fear based on certain financial reports.

It's important to realize that you can do all the right things—get out of debt, have a solid retirement plan, and keep a good amount of liquid money available—and still not be able to compensate for an economic tsunami that comes your way courtesy of these currency traders. Many people in these Asian nations had a personally healthy financial situation and lost it literally overnight. Many saw a lifetime of economic well-doing get wiped out in a moment through no personal or financial mistakes of their own. World traders run this mountain, not by consensus or strategy, but primarily through fears, rumors, and confidences.

World traders also greatly affect economics through stocks and shares—especially those traded on Wall Street. Just as speculation can create overreactions in the currency trade, daily stock exchanges can turn volatile at a moment's notice. Traders speculate on the value of a company's stock based on reports, reads on those reports, and future speculations of a trend. Instead of nations, various corporations and businesses are affected—and, of course, individuals and families further down the pike. Enron, for example, collapsed because it was discovered that its internal financial health picture had been doctored to look much better that it was. Investors realized they had over-valued their holdings and began selling off their shares. The massive devaluation that resulted caused many to go from financial security to financial devastation almost overnight. In this case, the crisis seems justified because of the company's internal financial misdeeds. But trade dynamics can also devastate a well-run corporation simply through perceptions and fears. To compound the uncertainty, a company's collapse always causes ripple effects that can potentially topple other businesses. The power of traders is profound.

As if these situations weren't troubling enough, Wall Street has other factors in play. Hedge funds are not subject to normal trade regulations; slush funds manipulate economic outlook; harder to explain factors such as residuals and derivatives expose the entire economic picture as a house of cards just waiting to be blown over. That's even without going into the potential risks of political hot topics like the national debt and personal consumer debt—or the fact that the U.S. Social Security system is pretty much a glorified Ponzi scheme that, without some kind of overhaul, has no mathematical possibility of surviving. (Thanks in part to the nearly fifty million abortions since *Roe v. Wade* that wiped out the next generation of providers for this fund.)[2]

Though the economy is a complex mountain, I believe it operates on easy-to-understand premises. Simplistically, it operates out of the law of supply and demand. Earlier I stated that the economy's health is determined by the proper balance of the production of resources, the distribution of resources, and the consumption of resources. The complication to this equation is that no resources have an actual determined value. They only have perceived value. This makes all resources subject to changes in value. They are tied into both actual and perceived supply and demand.

The ancient Incas had so much gold that they only valued it as much as we might value a tin can. They made gutters and pots for plants out of it. When Pizarro showed up and brought the rest of the world's demand for gold, its value suddenly rose dramatically.

My friends in Venezuela have told me they can get a full tank of gas for a dollar. In the U.S., one full tank can cost more than fifty dollars. Their abundance of gas brings the local price down, while they continue to take advantage of the global demand for fuel. But even this fuel is not a certain resource. Tomorrow an alternative fuel solution could be discovered and the world's economy would be thrown into major upheaval. Someone could discover that a teaspoon of a certain chemical, when mixed with water and baking soda, functions the same as oil on current vehicles. Or alternative fuel sources could prompt the invention of new types of engines. Either way, the resulting tsunami would transform the economy.

The point to remember is that no resource has a guaranteed value. Precious metals and jewels are treasured because they are scarce. Diamonds aren't valuable because they are diamonds, but because the demand for them exceeds what is known of their supply. Retirement accounts, mutual funds, gold, diamonds, oil, stocks, bank accounts, and even real estate are subject to forces beyond our control that could cause us to lose everything of value. A national crisis could cause the government to issue an edict confiscating all properties. This point is true at all levels, and if we are going to target this mountain as an inheritance, we need to understand that. Some of these scenarios may seem unlikely, but they are fairly common in many countries where governments step in and nationalize businesses and even homes. A friend of mine in Nicaragua had his family's mansion and plantations nationalized by the president in office at that time. Nothing—absolutely nothing—is a guaranteed asset if the right situation were to occur. Some assets are more secure than others, but nothing is certain. God has promised to shake everything that can be shaken.

God's instruction to us in 1 Timothy 6:17 is given with good reason: "Command those who are rich in this present age not to be haughty, nor to trust in uncertain riches but in the living God, who gives us richly all things to enjoy." My intention has been to shake your confidence in any present asset you may have. Of course, we have an unshakeable asset that we'll discuss later.

WHO CURRENTLY RULES THE ECONOMY?

The next great enemy nation mentioned in Deuteronomy 7 is the Canaanites, who represent those who currently dominate the mountain of economy. The Promised Land was often called Canaan for short, and we still understand the word *Canaan* as including some sort of financial boon (milk and honey and fruitfulness). *Canaanite* in Hebrew can be translated as "merchant, trader, and trafficker," and also "to be humbled, brought low, or to be under subjection." The word *Cana* means "zealous." Together, these words paint a picture of greed and poverty. The Canaanites on this mountain are working to either get people to be over-zealous in their trading and trafficking or to subject them to poverty—or both. These Canaanites of greed and poverty are opposed to anyone living in God's provision.

One of God's names is Jehovah-Jireh, which means "the Lord my provider." When we buy into the Canaanites' philosophy, we either live under the banner of financial hopelessness or the banner of financial euphoria. When we choose Jehovah-Jireh, we live under the banner of the Lord's provision. God's heart is for every person and every nation to live under His provision. He delights in providing for His children.

The Canaanites on this mountain oppose Him and us by putting us under a constant stressor of needing more and more without ever being content, or by setting up circumstances where survival itself is imperiled. And these goals feed each other; often the Canaanite of greed will open the door for one to experience another Canaanite spirit, poverty. The same spirits that cause starvation in Africa also cause Westerners to be spiritually lost in materialism. They are there to assist in supplanting God as provider. They prefer to release humiliating lack and suffering, but if God is so generous that He can't be stopped, then they try to twist the blessing into a pitfall of materialism. Though money and resources are a blessing from God, the zeal for those resources is the root of all kinds of evil.

WHO IS KING OF THE CANAANITES?

By looking for the king, we are seeking to identify the demonic principality that sits atop this mountain and uses the Canaanites of greed and poverty for his own means. I believe that this principality is Mammon, or Babylon.

> No servant can serve two masters; for either he will hate the one and love the other, or else he will be loyal to the one and despise the other. You cannot serve God and mammon.
>
> —LUKE 16:13

Mammon wrestles for God's seat in your life. He tells you he is actually your source for all true provision, and therefore for all peace and happiness. He is so deceptive and his web is so intriguing that most of us are caught up in it to some degree. Mammon's influence in us shows up as an excessive desire for money and wealth—in other words, greed.

> For the love of money is a root of all kinds of evil, for which some have strayed from the faith in their greediness, and pierced themselves through with many sorrows.
>
> —1 TIMOTHY 6:10

Paul, who lived in the era of New Testament Christianity many of us wish for, acknowledged that the seductiveness of greed had already caused some great losses in the church of that day. Love of money is a sign that someone is under the influence of Mammon, or Babylon. If the idea of money is euphoric to you, you are still in some measure under that influence. This is extremely important to determine because you can't take a mountain from a spirit under whose influence you function. If you grabbed this book and went straight to this chapter, you might still need some deliverance from this spirit. The exception would be if God instructed you to read this chapter specifically.

> After these things I saw another angel coming down from heaven, having great authority and the earth was illuminated with his glory. And he cried mightily with a loud voice, saying, "Babylon the great is fallen, is fallen…For all the nations have drunk of the wine of the wrath of her fornication, the kings of the earth have committed fornication with her, and the merchants of the earth have become rich through the abundance of her luxury."
> —REVELATION 18:1–3

This passage speaks of a time when the economic system of this world will collapse. Wealth itself won't collapse, but the present system of trader (Canaanite) domination will. The merchants of the earth are the traders. According to this passage, the Lord compares this system to fornication; it's unfaithful for anyone to look somewhere other than Him for provision. Now let's read the warning to us who are His people:

> And I heard another voice from heaven, saying, "Come out of her, my people, lest you share in her sins, and lest you receive of her plagues. For her sins have reached to heaven, and God has remembered her iniquities. Render to her just as she rendered to you, and repay her double according to her works; in the cup which she has mixed, mixed double for her."
> —REVELATION 18:4–6

God's plea to his people to "come out" is a call to extricate ourselves from being under this principality and the system it has created. In order to fully take this mountain, we will have to come out from under the influence of Babylon. The fact that the mark of the beast is an economic mark is very significant. (See Revelation 13:17–18.) Babylon's final judgment wraps up God's plan on Earth in the end times.

Babylon means "confusion by mixing." That's why scripture says she will be repaid double for the cup she has mixed. She serves a seductive wine, and even God's people can be intoxicated by it. Mammon and Babylon represent the power atop the Mountain of wealth, which must be dispossessed. (For more enlightening information on what Babylon represents, read the rest of Revelation 18.)

THE IMPORTANT ROLE OF PROPHETS

The five-fold ministry gift of prophet carries a very important role in the taking of the mountain of economy. Scripture speaks of a future transfer of wealth: "You shall eat of the riches of the Gentiles [nations]" (Isaiah 61:6) and, "The wealth of the Gentiles [nations] shall come to you" (Isaiah 60:5).

Many have speculated on how that will happen. Some people today are coming up with "apostolic" strategies for pulling this off. All of the strategies I've heard about involve using the wisdom of the world and learning how to exploit Babylon's system. Somehow, I don't think this is the way that it is going to take place. That seems a lot like an Ishmael solution—accepting the promise of God but exerting the arm of the flesh to perform it. Strategies that are based on Babylon's system in order to exploit it are destined to collapse whenever Babylon collapses. That's not how God establishes His kingdom.

I believe I have both some biblical insight as well as some personal history that can shed light on the role of prophetic ministry in taking this mountain. The scriptural principle is found in the 2 Chronicles 20:20 when King Jehoshaphat sent the Levites into battle in front of the army: "Believe in the LORD your God, and you shall be established; believe in His prophets, and you shall prosper" (2 Chronicles 20:20). The word for "prosper" is the same Hebrew word used to describe Joseph as a prosperous man in Genesis 39:2. Our tendency is to spiritualize this word, but it definitely implies material wealth. So, according to Jehoshaphat's statement, a key to prosperity lies in the role of prophets.

That's why scripture is so pointed in identifying false prophets as those who go after "the sin of Balaam." (See Jude 1:11 and 2 Peter 2:15.) A false prophet is motivated by profit, regardless of whether his prophetic gift is otherwise valid. A true prophet does not function out of money motives, which is why the principle of having to come out from under the influence of a mountain in order to have authority over it is so relevant in this case.

PERSONAL TESTIMONIES

I have seen the Lord move in some amazing ways as it relates to the prophetic uncovering of wealth. Jesus said, "the kingdom of heaven is like a treasure hidden in a field" (Matt. 13:44). The next verse reiterates the point: "Again, the kingdom of heaven is like a merchant seeking beautiful pearls" (Matt. 13:45). This is a guiding principle for how I practice and teach on prophetic ministry. It doesn't take a prophetic gift to see the field (dirt) where a treasure lies. That's just a gift of obvious—seeing the negative situation of an individual, situation, or even a nation. How the reign of heaven is activated on the earth is in using the prophetic gift to discover the treasure or pearl that's hidden there. As we call the treasure forth, it surfaces from the dirt.

This has multiple applications. The destiny of people and nations is their treasure. This was the challenge the Lord laid out before Ezekiel: can you see an exceedingly great army in a valley full of very dry bones? (See Ezekiel 37:1–10.) As he prophesied, the "treasure" began to manifest.

Several years ago, I went into the jungle city of Saposoa, Peru. It was my first visit into an extremely poor and beaten-up city. Years of narco-terrorism and the government strike-back against it had left the city very isolated, needy, and destitute. I asked to meet with the mayor and was received by him. He shared with me the challenges that he was facing in his city, and in particular the difficulty of getting people who used to make easy money with coca growing to commit to working much harder for less money in cultivating coffee, cacao, bananas, or rice. I then began telling this mayor, who was not a Christian, that he had been chosen for such a time as this and that God honored his good heart toward his people.

I then told him some things prophetically: "God is going to help you with the economy of your city. There will be things discovered that have never been discovered before. These things will bless the economy of your city. Also I think a lost city of the Incas or Indian civilization is going to be found around here and is going to garner this place much attention." I explained that I was telling him these things so that when they occurred, he would give credit to God for His help. I then asked if I could pray with him, which I did. Amazingly, he then turned to me and said, "I'm having this day declared a historic day in the city of Saposoa. I am going to have a plaque put up in City Hall that declares you to be illustrious guests of this city. I am going to give you the keys to the city and I would like you to be with me tomorrow when a city parade goes by—and would you please pray for my wife, as she has a nervous disorder?" I prayed for her and she was healed. I found out later that when I laid hands on him, he was healed of a migraine headache.

Part of the incredible story of Saposoa is that within eighteen months, two salt mines, one thermal spring, one scenic waterfall, a zinc mine, and a silver mine were discovered. The area was not known for any of these things. In addition, a forty-square-kilometer "lost city" was found thirty miles from where we had met. The archaeologist Gene Savoy had been searching for it for decades. It was named La Gran Saposoa (meaning the Great Saposoa) and has made world news several times.

My next time into the city, we were received at the entrance of the city by all of its leaders. All city school kids were in their marching uniforms, and they led a parade into town, where I was again given the keys to the city and welcomed to freely have meetings in the central square. Over a thousand gave their lives to the Lord, and hundreds were healed in meetings in the central square during the next couple of days. The mayor subsequently gave his life to the Lord. He has even come to the U.S. and stayed with my family for three days. Truly the kindness of the Lord leads to repentance.

I strongly believe that one of the reasons the Lord responded so powerfully and quickly to this prophetic word was because of the mayor's immediate and profound acceptance of it. His migraine's disappearance was a sign to him, so he embraced the prophecy. He honored me as if the word I spoke had already happened—long before anything actually did.

Largely because of the favor God gave me in this far out jungle city, I was invited to speak at a prestigious national pastors' conference in Lima, the capital. I took the opportunity to tell them the Saposoa story. I also told them that the Lord was going to transform their national economy and take all sectors of Peru's society. He would invade government and begin to place believers in many key positions of society. I told them I saw Peru becoming a very wealthy nation in South America, a lending nation rather than a debtor nation, and would one day send many missionaries to the Middle East.

The pastors at this conference were simultaneously excited and doubtful. They *wanted* to believe, but they had felt oppressed for so long—like financially hopeless Canaanites—that it seemed too good to be true. I acknowledged to them that I saw their doubt. Then I told them that the Lord would give them a sign so they could believe: a significant gold mine would soon be discovered in Trujillo, a city of one million that was not known for mining. I was led to tell them that this mine would not be the actual financial blessing, but rather a sign God would use to trigger their faith so that they could believe for the greater blessings to come.

Three months later, I visited Trujillo for only the second time in my life. I was on a radio station where the interviewer asked me what I saw prophetically for them as a city. I shared some things that the Lord had given me and then also told them that I had just prophesied three months prior that a significant gold mine would be discovered in Trujillo. I told them I had seen it clearer while now in town, that it was a very large gold mine, and that when it was discovered they could know it was a sign that the rest of what I had just spoken was going to take place. On the air, my chauffeur, who happened to also work for a mining company, interrupted me. "Prophet," he said, "we have just discovered the largest gold mine in the history of Peru! It was just in the last couple of weeks, and the initial 'scrapings' to come out of it were valued at $176 million." Everyone was so excited that I was kept on the radio an extra hour or so. The mayor of the city ended up calling in.

Some time after that, I was back in Lima reminding the pastors and churches of the prophetic sign of the gold mine discovery in Trujillo. I reminded them that this wasn't even the financial blessing yet—that "until the Lord removes the corrupt infrastructure, much will still be wasted." I then prophesied that the Lord was going to help their weak faith even more by soon allowing an even larger gold mine to be discovered and that this too would not even be the coming blessing that I anticipated. Shortly thereafter, the new largest gold mine in Peru was discovered. The mining rights were reported to have been sold for forty billion dollars! That's for just the rights to mine it; the government still gets a percentage from whatever the mine yields. It is being projected that from this one mine alone, the standard of living of Peru will go up every year for the next twenty-five years. And this is just a sign of the blessing yet to come.

I have not made it a point to call forth natural resources prophetically. As I have traveled throughout several South American nations, my passion and prophetic words are almost always geared towards something more spiritual. Yet inevitably I have found myself announcing the future discovery of a "treasure" as a sign. I once gave a long prophetic word for Costa Rica and said the sign would be "gold discovered in the northeast of the nation." The following week, someone sent me a newspaper headline reporting the largest gold discovery in Costa Rica. In Nicaragua, I said a diamond-like special stone would be discovered in the mountains near the capital. I was informed that it had, in fact, just happened. In Honduras, I saw a vision of an oil rig in a city and told the pastor to look for the discovery of oil to be announced. He told me I was a little late, as it had just been reported. Of course, I had no idea that had just happened. I could go one with many examples, but you get the point.

Prophetic ministry can surface treasures. "Believe His prophets, and you shall prosper" (2 Chron. 20:20).

Scripture says that the world not only will be filled with the glory of the Lord, but that it already is. (See Isaiah 6:3 and Habakkuk 2:14.) One of the definitions of *glory* is "riches"—all kinds. God's glory—in every aspect of creation, including the material—is woven into this world, everywhere. Innumerable treasures are waiting to be discovered and prophetically called out of obscurity—an entirely new fuel source, simple natural cures for deadly diseases, and so on. These treasures are not the real treasure, of course. The real treasure is Jehovah-Jireh, who can call forth every source of provision for those who trust in Him. Hearing His voice is the asset beyond assets for the last days, when everything that can be shaken *will* be shaken. If we are connected to the ultimate unshakeable asset, it won't matter when Babylon collapses.

That's why we are to passionately desire the gifts of the Holy Spirit (see 1 Corinthians 12), especially the gift of prophecy, which Paul called the greatest of spiritual gifts (see 1 Corinthians 14:1). This is why the coming revolution must be an Elijah Revolution—a prophetic renewal unleashed across the earth. Above all other gifts, the voice of the Lord must be restored to His church.

We have to remember that if we have a powerful Jehovah-Jireh account, we don't really need a powerful bank account on Earth. It doesn't matter if we lose all of our funds, our lands, our gold, our cash—whatever. He can provide for us from His very self. We don't need to hoard and justify it as wise planning for our kids or the future. Anything He doesn't say to keep in a savings plan of sorts should be used to presently expand the kingdom of God. At some point or another, we are going to have to wean ourselves from dependence on this world's economic system, and the sooner the better. "Come out of her My people, that ye be not partakers of her sins" (Rev. 18:4, KJV). The issue isn't pulling our money and stocks out, it's pulling our hearts and souls out.

God can bless financially in an infinite number of ways, including extracting from Babylon's wealth if He so desires. Paul's command in

1 Timothy 6:17 is "don't trust in uncertain riches." Instead, trust in Him who is truly rich.

> You shall remember the LORD your God, for it is He who gives
> you power to get wealth, that He may establish His covenant.
> —DEUTERONOMY 8:18

The specific power God gives us is not to make wealth but to *get* it. That means He does all the work and strategizing, and we just receive it. The transfer of wealth is not going to come through our Christian brainpower. In most cases, we will just fall into it. A Christian never needs to pursue wealth, only the One who is wealthy. If we don't get this point, the wealth itself will compete for the seat of God in our lives.

JOSEPH AND EGYPT'S WEALTH

Earlier, I related some of my personal stories of seeing how the prophetic gift surfaces treasures. We can see also the same principle in the life of Joseph, the story of a man who, entirely on the back of his prophetic gift, was placed in charge of all of world's resources. His gift in interpreting dreams gave him access that he could have had in no other way. No amount of business degrees or financial training could compare with the asset of hearing and interpreting what God was saying. Much is being said today about the Lord raising a Joseph Company that the Lord will entrust with great end-time wealth. Though I believe this is true, this company will only be made up of those who recognize what the actual asset is—hearing His voice.

ELIJAH AND ELISHA

The prophets Elijah and Elisha were used several times to release God's provision. Elijah released the rain that ended the drought. Elisha provided the widow with all the oil she could handle to offset the dire financial predicament she was in. I really like the story of

Elisha and how he broke the famine over Samaria that was so severe that even children were being eaten:

> Then Elisha said, "Hear the word of the LORD, Thus says the LORD: "Tomorrow about this time a seah of fine flour shall be sold for a shekel, and two seahs of barley for a shekel at the gate of Samaria." So an officer on whose hand the king leaned answered the man of God and said, "Look, if the LORD would make windows in heaven, could this thing be?" And he said, "In fact, you shall see it with your eyes, but you shall not eat of it."
> —2 KINGS 7:1–2

Elisha's prophecy of supernatural provision was utterly unbelievable to this officer. That very day, dove's droppings were selling for five shekels of silver! And now fine flour was going to sell for one shekel of silver! How could this be possible? And how could it happen in one day? The answer is that the prophetic can access supernatural treasure. "Believe His prophets, and you shall prosper" (2 Chron. 20:20). Later that day, God caused the Syrian army to hear the noise of chariots, horses, and a great army; and they ran off and left all their tents, donkeys, horses, and supplies. There was gold, silver, food, and everything. The officer who doubted was trampled by the people who rushed to get all the supplies. He saw the abundance but never benefited from it.

One of the Lord's favorite trademarks is allowing us to spoil the enemy. He can provide manna from heaven, water from the rock, and many loaves and fishes from hardly anything. But what He really likes to do is turn over to us—with no significant effort on our part—the wealth of the nations, just as He did when Israel plundered Egypt's wealth during the Exodus.

In Matthew 17:27, Jesus further modeled God's ability to extract wealth from wherever He wants when a fish provided enough gold for His and Peter's temple tax. This prophetic gifting will be the greatest source for changing the economical balance of power in these last days.

LEVELS OF THE MOUNTAIN

At the top of the mountain of economy/wealth sit several nations, institutions, and people. The United States and other so-called G-8 nations (Canada, France, Germany, Italy, Japan, Russia, and the United Kingdom) represent 65 percent of the world's economy and form a very powerful bloc. The oil industry is currently high on the mountain. Bill Gates and Warren Buffet, as two of the world's richest men, are very influential. All of that, of course, is subject to sudden and dramatic change.

The geographical top of this mountain is New York City, primarily because of Wall Street. The perspective of Revelation 18 could easily apply to New York City; in fact, the 9/11 terrorist attack came eerily close to what is described in that chapter. World currency traders obviously affect the world economy at this time, and any concentrated blocs working together in that realm can theoretically manipulate the wealth of the nations.

Further down the mountain are regional and local considerations—in a globally interconnected economy, even less significant stock markets can affect all of them—but clearly the top of the mountain is able to manipulate and dominate the entire mountain. A great place of influence at lower levels is being able to affect the say-so as local budgets are applied. This would include key financial advisory roles to governors, mayors, and other local leadership. This influence not only has local impact but also can substantially impact other nations.

WHAT THE BIBLE SAYS ABOUT THE ECONOMY

Obviously, the Bible is very extensive in covering the topic of wealth, and we have already gone through a substantial number of passages. We will add a handful of scriptures to further establish its voice into these matters. Haggai 2:6–9 is a very significant and insightful prophecy:

> For thus says the LORD of hosts: "Once more (it is a little while) I will shake heaven and earth, the sea and dry land; and I will shake all nations, and they shall come to the Desire of All

Nations, and I will fill this temple with glory," says the LORD of hosts. "The silver is Mine and the gold is Mine," says the Lord of hosts. "The glory of this latter temple shall be greater than the former," says the LORD of hosts. "And in this place I will give peace," says the Lord of hosts.

This passage covers an array of end-time perspectives. Five times God is called the LORD of hosts, which speaks to His appearance in the latter days as Ruler of the nations and Commander of His army. His hosts include Elijah revolutionaries. When He comes in takeover mode, He will shake everything that can be shaken. Hebrews 12:25–29 builds on this concept:

See that you do not refuse Him who speaks. For if they did not escape who refused Him who spoke on earth, much more shall we not escape if we turn away from Him who speaks from heaven, whose voice then shook the earth; but now He has promised saying, "Yet once more I shake not only the earth, but also heaven." Now this, "Yet once more," indicates the removal of those things that are being shaken, as of things that are made, that the things which cannot be shaken may remain. Therefore since we are receiving a kingdom, which cannot be shaken, let us have grace, by which we may serve God acceptably with reverence and godly fear. For our God is a consuming fire.

The reason He is shaking everything that can be shaken is so that only the unshakeable—the kingdom of God—will remain. We, His children, are meant to receive His unshakeable kingdom. The more that happens, the closer Isaiah 2:2 comes to fulfillment. The mountain of the Lord's house is established over every other mountain.

For this reason, Babylon must be shaken until it collapses, for it is an economic system built on something other than trust in God. All that is not centered in God is shakable and will ultimately collapse. Haggai speaks of this shaking as causing all nations to recognize that

God is "the Desire of All Nations" (Hag. 2:7). God will be treasured above riches around the world!

In the midst of Haggai's description of this awesome end-time scenario is the phrase, "The silver is Mine, and the gold is Mine" (Hag. 2:8). In other words, all wealth is His. We are not to come to the Lord motivated by His wealth, but these things are added when we seek first His kingdom.

When God shakes the nations and reveals His kingdom, His temple will be filled with unprecedented glory. It will be filled with peace, regardless of what rages outside. As the Antichrist pushes for dependence on an economic mark of the beast, God will reveal that the silver is His and the gold is His. Only those who are temporarily and foolishly deceived by the beast will choose to go down with Babylon.

The mark of the beast may not be some future visible sign, as many suppose. It may be an already-existing reality of those who trust in mammon. First God will shake that mark out of His own household, as it's a significant problem among those in His own temple. He comes as a "refiners fire" into His own temple (Mal. 3:2–3), cleansing it of mammon. This is the prophetic picture Jesus gave us in John 2 when He cleansed the temple:

> Now the Passover of the Jews was at hand, and Jesus went up to Jerusalem. And He found in the temple those who sold oxen and sheep and doves, and the money changers doing business. When He had made a whip out of cords, He drove them all out of the temple, with the sheep and the oxen, and poured out the changers' money and overturned the tables.
>
> —JOHN 2:13–15

Jesus' historic cleansing of the temple is familiar to most of us, and we get the basic premise that the Lord does not want His temple to be turned into a center of greed and moneymaking. However, the next two verses indicate that there's more to it than first meets the eye:

> And He said to those who sold doves, "Take these things away! Do not make My Father's house a house of merchandise!" Then

> His disciples remembered that it was written, "Zeal for your
> house has eaten Me up."
>
> —JOHN 2:16–17

Those who sold oxen, sheep, and doves were all driven out, but the text goes out of its way to point out the target of Jesus' harshest words: "those who sold doves." Doves, of course, are a prophetic picture of the Holy Spirit. They can be a symbol for a specific anointing of God. In effect, the Lord is saying He will come in judgment against those who "merchandise the anointing" because it defiles His temple.

I believe that much of this merchandising of the anointing is going on in His temple today, and it really must be cleaned up. There's nothing wrong with selling books, tapes, magazines, CDs, and so on; that's not in itself evidence of merchandising the anointing. But the step from offering resources to merchandising the Spirit is very small and easy to take. We can start out with a pure desire to distribute the good things God has entrusted us with, which does cost money. But at some point profit can become a motivating factor in deciding how and where we minister. We move from an acceptable distribution method to a bottom-line business. When it crosses that line, we become a merchandiser of the anointing and put ourselves in the Lord's upcoming line of fire. Jesus warned us of "the deceitfulness of riches" for good reason (Mark 4:19). We must come out of Babylon, or we will suffer for her sins.

A MULTI-PRONGED APPROACH

Taking this mountain of economy/wealth will clearly entail a very multi-faceted strategy. First, we must sanctify ourselves by being cleansed of the love of money. If we are going to be a part of taking this mountain, we must first "come out of her" (Rev. 18:4–6). Simple self-tests—for example, do we readily and eagerly offer our firstfruit offerings to the Lord?—can help us see if we're ready to begin tackling this mountain. A natural giftedness in financial matters is not a sign of a calling. In fact, it may lend itself to a greater temptation to be merchandise-motivated rather than kingdom-motivated. That can be overcome, but it requires some profound cleansing by the Lord. The prophetic ministry is valuable in confirming whether or not someone is called to operate on this mountain.

A person can be called to this mountain in many different capacities—as an intercessor or in having a significant net worth that's given over to the Lord—and can lead to promotion in this area. But I believe the primary call for most who will influence this mountain is to be influencers of those who have the actual resources. Even as Joseph didn't really have Egypt's resources—they belonged to Pharaoh—but rather the influence over how they were collected and distributed, so will God fill this mountain with those who are to manage the resources of others. Whether one uses his or her own resources or has stewardship over the wealth of others, kingdom motivation must be the driving passion. Whenever a desire for profit exceeds a desire for the kingdom to come, that person cannot be greatly used by the Lord on this mountain.

THE PRAYER STRATEGY

As I present these strategies, both for action and for prayer, I'm very aware that this is not an exhaustive approach. I've been shown a few things, and more revelation will come to those who actually lock into the Lord and begin the journey of taking their mountain.

From an intercessory standpoint, covering all those on the top of the mountain in prayer is an obvious starting point. One can receive an intercessory assignment to pray that Satan would not succeed in the destruction of nations through the daily world currency trades. Before the time when the world's economic system collapses, Satan will prematurely try to cause death, destruction, lawlessness, and disaster by manipulating financial devastation. We want to work to stop that. In intercession, we first want to find *who* the objects of his assignments are and then *what* the specific strategy of the assignment is. This field is so wide open for prayer initiatives that prophetic directives can be very valuable. As we become more tuned into God and what He is doing upon the earth, we will better know how to pray.

The Action Strategy

The action strategy is an all-points penetration of everything currently at the top of the mountain of wealth, as well as Spirit-led foresight into whatever is already on its way to the top. We need to come up with new commodities (a new fuel source, for example) and business practices, and we need to back people and organizations ascending this hill. Mainly we need to know that the Lord is working toward the removal of all that is shakable, and as God's people, we must be ready to step in as the "displacers" after He's done with the heavy lifting of the assignment: shaking everything that can be shaken.

One very significant point of action that I've seen is that the Lord intends to greatly use and promote righteous charitable relief organizations. We will soon have so many natural disasters throughout the world that those accustomed to responding will experience emotional and financial burnout. The Lord will bankroll and bless those who are called by Him to step into the gap. They will be a fulfillment of Isaiah 61:4: "They shall rebuild the old ruins, They shall raise up the former desolations, And they shall repair the ruined cities, The desolations of many generations."

Those who have kingdom understanding in this area will see that these coming relief organizations will actually carry great privilege and authority to promote and initiate righteous nation building. National governments will not have the luxury of placing terms on those bringing relief. The desperation will be so great and the nations' leadership will be so overwhelmed that they will have to turn to the mountain of the Lord's house for help.

Some of these relief agencies of the kingdom will be able to operate outside of Babylon's financial system. They will be outrageously prosperous, while much of the world lives in scarcity. They will, in fact, be called on to bankroll entire nations as these nations come out of the metaphoric grave. God owns the silver and the gold, and those among His people who are kingdom-minded will grow increasingly wealthy as times get more difficult and as they wean themselves from Babylon. As the fear of the Lord becomes a reality around the world, multiple

"Josephs" will be raised up in many nations to oversee their extreme makeovers.

Get ready for a dramatic acceleration to be released upon God's servants who understand the kingdom of God. Christians will in fact continue to be a part of the problem if they don't understand the kingdom of God and its relentless advance on planet Earth. No Christian who embraces an "abandon the planet" theology will be of much use to the big picture of what God wants to do on Earth. They can still have a relationship with God and go to heaven when they die, but upon arriving there they will be struck by how thoroughly they were deceived by a doctrine of demons. I will say it again: "In the latter days…the mountain of the Lord's house shall be established on the top of the mountains…And all nations shall flow [come running] to it" (Isa. 2:2–3).

According to the book of Daniel, "The people who know their God shall be strong and carry out great exploits" (Daniel 11:32)—even while the Antichrist is setting up his throne. According to Webster's dictionary, exploits are "notable or heroic acts." That's our destiny in the midst of the supposed high, exalted days of the Antichrist. There is no waiting downtime for a believer. The instruction in Luke 19:13 is, "Occupy till I come" (KJV). He will return not for a desperate, beaten-up, defeated church, but for a victorious church who has fulfilled her occupation.

The mountain of economy and wealth is extremely significant as an occupation that must, and will, be done. Mammon has been ruling, and the Canaanites of greed and poverty have long been dominating. It will all change as Elijah revolutionaries hear the call of God and take this mountain.

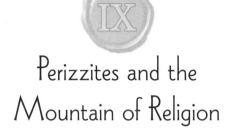

Perizzites and the
Mountain of Religion

THE MOUNTAIN OF religion is the mountain that we as Christians are most familiar with. It is perhaps the only battlefield that some of us have recognized. We've accidentally advanced very far on this mountain, but a significant battle awaits us. I say "accidentally" because we've primarily advanced on this mountain through bottom-line decisions for Christ. We've filled the mountain with people, but we've under-informed most on the mountain as to what the mission is.

WHAT IS RELIGION?

The definition of *religion* is "the service and worship of God, or the supernatural."

We have learned a lot about religion in a negative context as that which is ritual and not real, but there is a pure and undefiled religion that is good. The four great religions on the earth are Christianity (2.1 billion followers), Islam (1.2 billion), Hinduism (900 million), and Buddhism (376 million). Other major religions are Chinese traditional/folk religion (394 million), which mixes various strains of Taoism, Confucianism, and Buddhism. African folk religions that often mix the occult and Christianity/Catholicism are practiced by more than 100 million. There are 14 million Jews, and millions spread out among other religious groups.[1]

Christianity is the fastest growing religion in the world, with Charismatic/Pentecostal being the fastest growing group within Christianity. More than 700 million Holy Spirit-filled Christians are in the world, and their numbers and influence are growing exponentially, particularly so in South America and Africa.

WHO RULES THE MOUNTAIN OF RELIGION?

Next in our list of the Deuteronomy 7 nations to be dispossessed are the Perizzites. The Perizzites' name means "unwalled, rustic dweller." They lived in the hill country of the tribes of Judah and Joseph.

> Then the children of Joseph spoke to Joshua saying, "Why have you given us only one lot and one share to inherit, since we are a great people, inasmuch as the LORD has blessed us until now?" So Joshua answered them, "If you are a great people, then go up to the forest country and clear a place for yourself there in the land of the Perizzites and the giants, since the mountains of Ephraim are too confined for you."
> —JOSHUA 17:14–15

What the land of the Perizzites and the giants represents, for our purposes, is idolatry In Scripture, idolatry was always entrenched in the "high places," the last holdouts in Israel's struggles against false worship. This land of the Perizzites was also called the land of the giants, indicating that idolatry creates religious giants that need to be removed. That their name means "unwalled" denotes that they have no protection. That they are "rustic dwellers" means that they also experience limited provision.

Idolatry strips people of their protection and their provision. War and famine are common trademarks of people locked into a system of false worship. History shows that as a people and a nation eradicate idolatry and turn to worship of the true and living God, a better economy and less fighting soon follows. Idolatry is particularly insidious because the very things it causes—death and lack—are the very things it purports to remedy.

120

THE MEANING OF IDOLATRY

The word *idolatry* means:

1. the worship of a physical object as a god;
2. immoderate attachment or devotion to something.

The word *idol* means "an object of worship, a likeness of something, a false god, a pretender, an impostor." An idolater is therefore "a person who intensely and often blindly admires someone or something that is not an object of worship." This, of course, all adds up to religious deception.

THE IDOLATRY IN ISLAM

The central idolatry in Islam is the worship of Allah. For Muslims, he represents a perspective of who God really is; but this perspective is clearly not the God of the Bible, nor the God who is the Father of Jesus. Also, Muslims's staunch anti-trinitarianism is a rejection of Jesus and the Holy Spirit as expressions of God. Whoever they intend to worship, their actual god seems to be the prince of Persia that Daniel dealt with in the Old Testament.

The prophet Mohammed is also idolized. Reason has little or no value in reaching some Muslims for Christ. However, once Muslims feel the presence and power of the Holy Spirit, they toss out their arguments against Christianity. Multitudes in the Middle East are coming to the Lord as He reveals Himself to them either in a dream or personally.

THE IDOLATRY IN HINDUISM

The idolatry in Hinduism is so widespread, extreme, and extensive, that it is well-established as the most idolatrous religion on the planet—estimated to have 330 million gods. Hindus generally sell out their soul to a vast array of demons who are thus empowered to rule among them, causing lack of provision and protection—not to

THE SEVEN MOUNTAIN PROPHECY

mention deceiving them into hell, the ultimate lack of provision and protection. Whereas a Muslim will be very spiritually narrow—only Allah and his prophet Mohammed are accepted—most Hindus are open to everything. They will accept any and every new god that could grant them some favor. The biggest obstacle with them is not found in getting them to make a decision for the Lord, but in getting them to eliminate all the other gods in their lives. Their idolatrous practices make them virtual spiritual "swinging doors;" anything can come in, and anything can go out. On the positive side, when a Hindu has a true encounter with God's power, he or she responds with extreme devotion to Him.

THE IDOLATRY IN BUDDHISM

Buddhism is also filled with a notorious amount of idols and images, and may only be marginally behind Hinduism in that respect. Yet it is theoretically a very different religion in that it is officially nontheistic. However, any time idols and images are involved in your faith, you in fact are serving the demons behind those images. The greatest idol in Buddhism is probably self, and in effect this manifests as a religion of humanism. The goal is an enlightened state of *nirvana*, which is basically a glorification of humanity's utopian possibilities. But even nirvana ends in poverty and lack for the individual; the ultimate hope of Buddhism is to escape the cycles of pain and suffering by eventually becoming a non-self. Nirvana is a universal oneness in which the individual no longer exists.

This religion mixes very well with what we call New Age beliefs. At its core, its emphasis on the individual's path to salvation through works, meditations, and self-disciplines serves as an attempt to deify man. It espouses what we would all agree is good—peace, love, joy, and hope—but the problem is that it looks to some altered human state to bring that about. It attempts a path of salvation apart from Jesus, which of course is impossible. Buddhists tend to be open to experiment with new spiritual possibilities, and therefore can also be open to the Lord. But their resistance to Christianity is greater than that of Hindus, especially when they remind themselves that they are nontheistic.

OTHER FORMS OF IDOLATRY

Chinese traditional religions carry much of the same approach and feel as Buddhism. Enlightenment and wisdom are main emphases, especially with the influence of Confucianism added in, and good things like honor and nobility are mixed with idolatrous attitudes toward ancestors and wealth.

African traditional religions, which have also carried over to the Caribbean in voodoo and Santería, are much darker and more openly or obviously demonic. Witchcraft and bloodletting often mixed in with some token elements of Jesus and God. These are very much based on fear and infected with idolatry.

I've listed only the major religions of the world, as limitless expressions and variations are scattered everywhere and would be impossible to cover thoroughly. But in every case, the mountain of religion is full of idolatry.

THE KING OF THE PERIZZITES

The principality sitting atop this mountain of religion is the religious spirit. This demon is assigned to steal worship designated for God. Human beings innately know that there is a God and that we must approach Him in some fashion. The spirit of religion's job is to prostitute that God-placed homing device and lead the worship elsewhere. The following is his list of preferences on how to steal worship:

- Inspire open and intentional worship of Satan (Satanism)

- Divert worship to objects (idols) that originate in Satan's mind (secondary Satan worship)

- Direct worship to man himself (Satan doesn't get the worship but knows it displeases God)

- Make worship vague and symbolic, if God must be worshiped at all—and, if at all possible, minus Jesus

- If a real relationship with God through Jesus is present, then doctrinally eliminate the Holy Spirit

- If a real relationship with God through Jesus and the Holy Spirit is present, then eliminate His power manifestations (dispensationalism, cessationism)

- If a real relationship with God through Jesus that includes power manifestations of the Holy Spirit is present, then obstruct the theological understanding of just how close one can get to God, and how much authority we have been given on Earth (creating immobilized "rapture waiters")

The religious spirit will work at whatever level of commitment someone has in pursuing God. His job is to attach a *feeling* of religiosity to anything that is not direct worship of the Creator Himself. If we are relentless in our pursuit of God, this spirit will attempt to focus us on the good things of God to see if we'll pursue them instead of God Himself. He will try to form idols or stack idols at every turn to steal God's worship. If we won't worship an obvious idol, he'll work with his Perizzites to get us idolizing a Christian leader, a doctrine, a manifestation, spiritual gifts, or God's provision. Anything that he can lift up to block our view of the Lord is what he is all about. And he's very good at his job.

The spirit of religion is a master at getting even mature Spirit-filled believers to stall out in their worship. He will coax and induce us to stop and memorialize a mountaintop moment, a teaching, or an experience. (We often call this being stuck in an old wineskin.) Knowing that we are supposed to learn from history, the religious spirit will try to get us locked into old traditions. He is satisfied with whatever he can do to quench the Holy Spirit and His present-day emphasis and advance. If he can't keep us from salvation, he'll at least try to stop us there. If we insist on the power of the Holy Spirit, he'll work to restrict it only to tongues. If we insist on everything God has for us, he'll attempt to at least restrict our arena of operation by making us "Sunday Christians" who worship only in church. He uses any form of idolatry at every turn so that by whatever means necessary he gets our eyes off of God and steals our true worship.

This principality's power is not in his spiritual might but in his lies. When we believe his lies, we give him power. He most effectively operates undercover. Very few will choose to worship Satan as the devil he is, so he comes stealthily as an angel of light. Most of his doctrines that deceive the masses carry many elements of truth. He'll advocate all the characteristics of the fruit of the Holy Spirit if he can convince people that those characteristics are obtainable apart from the Spirit. His doctrines often cook a perfect loaf of bread that's spiked with deadly poison. Some New Age doctrines are almost completely right, except that they can be pulled off without Jesus or the Holy Spirit.

An example of this is peace. Peace is an important biblical characteristic, and any faith that advocates it sounds right. But humanly manufactured peace, which is just the denial of a stressor, does not compare to the "peace that passes understanding" that comes from our Prince of Peace. When you don't know that kind of peace is a real possibility, however, your ability to mask symptoms seems better than the raw pain you were feeling. The spirit of religion thrives where true, biblical, powerful Christianity isn't being modeled.

THE CENTRAL ROLE OF THE HOLY SPIRIT

It would take volumes to exhaustively cover the Holy Spirit's role and how it relates to all the ministries of the body of Christ. For our purposes, we won't be able to dot every *i* and cross every *t*, but we will make some important observations. I mentioned that the religious spirit thrives in the absence of true, biblical, powerful Christianity. When we model a Christianity that does not carry power, presence, and passion, then we're demonstrating a product that's so inferior that cheap counterfeits can thrive. All other religions on this mountain, whether Islam, Buddhism, or Hinduism, are easily displaceable when real, Holy Spirit-driven Christianity shows up.

Since the renewed attention on the Holy Spirit brought on one hundred years ago by the Azusa Street revival, Christianity has exploded across the globe like never before. As this last century has progressed, so too has a dramatic increase of Christian conversions. Nearly 70 percent of those ever saved in the history of the world have come to Christ since the Azusa outpouring of the Holy Spirit in 1906. More than 50 percent of those ever saved have come to Christ since 1948, which, not coincidentally, is the year that Israel again became a nation. More Muslims have come to the Lord since 1980 than in the thousand years before that. A high percentage of that growth has been since 9/11. In 1900, the ratio of Christians to non-Christians world-wide was 1 to 27. Now it's 1 to 2—33 percent of the world's population. (When trying to count only those who are truly born again, the ratio can drop as low as 1 to 5.) Any way we look at it, this last century has seen the Holy Spirit move in His people like never before, causing the mountain of religion to shake and its dark forces rapidly to be displaced.

Satan has been willing to concede to us a Father God up in heaven who theoretically loves us and is in charge. He has reluctantly put up with Jesus, who died for our sins so that we could one day make it to heaven. But what really bothers him is the dimension of God that the Holy Spirit brings to planet Earth. He's the One who brings us the presence, the power, and the passion of God. Without Him, our religion is for the most part dead—even with right doctrines on God and Jesus. The Godhead functions as a Trinity, and each member has a role in the redemption of man and establishing the kingdom of God on Earth. The Spirit is the agent of the Trinity specifically assigned to us in our time. As with most aspects of the Trinity, this is a mystery, but we are to go with what has been revealed. The Father sent Jesus, who, on the cross, paid the price for the redemption of man *and* all of creation. Jesus told His disciples that in addition to the work of redemption on the cross, His purpose was to send the Holy Spirit to help them.

These things I have spoken to you while being present with you. But the Helper, Holy Spirit, whom the Father will send in my name, He will teach you all things, and bring to your remembrance all things that I said to you.

—JOHN 14:25–26

When He, the Spirit of truth, has come, He will guide you into all truth; for He will not speak on His own authority, but whatever He hears He will speak; and He will tell you things to come.

—JOHN 16:13

Being assembled together with them, He commanded them not to depart from Jerusalem, but to wait for the Promise of the Father, "which," He said, "you have heard from me. For John truly baptized with water, but you shall be baptized with the Holy Spirit not many days from now…But you shall receive power when the Holy Spirit has come upon you, and you shall be witnesses to Me in Jerusalem, and in all Judea, and Samaria, and to the end of the earth."

—ACTS 1:4, 8

The reason Satan fights us so strenuously on the Holy Spirit is that the Spirit allows us to be all that the Father desires us to be. He's our teacher (John 14:25), He's our prophet (John 16:13), and He's our empowerer (Acts 1). The flip side of that is that without Him, we will *not* know things we should, we will *not* know things that are to come, and we will *not* have power. No wonder the spirit of religion wants the church to be content with a tame, theoretical Holy Spirit who does not actually manifest. This spirit tells us lies like, "The Holy Spirit is a gentleman," even though His very first manifestation in Acts 2 was as "a mighty rushing wind" that created all kinds of chaos. He'll tell us that "the Holy Spirit does not bring confusion," when Scripture shows quite a few examples of the opposite.

(Note: it is true that 1 Corinthians 14:33 says that God is not a God of confusion, but Paul was talking to a church where everyone competed to give prophecies and speak in tongues, disrupting the flow of the Spirit.) However, that does not mean that wherever we see confusion, we can say God isn't there. Jesus' disciples were often confused by what He said. The "foolishness of God" often confused the wise (1 Cor. 1:25), and the Spirit almost always defied people's expectations:

> There were dwelling in Jerusalem Jews, devout men, from every nation under heaven. And when this sound occurred, the multitude came together, and were confused…they were all amazed and marveled…so they were all amazed and perplexed, saying to one another, "Whatever could this mean?" Others mocking said, "They are full of new wine."
>
> —ACTS 2:5, 13

The Holy Spirit comes with a "new wineskin" and to ensure that we continue to stay new. When He first comes in a new measure, He breaks the existing wineskin. Devout men are always confused, amazed, and perplexed—and will inevitably judge the manifestations for not fitting the old wineskin. Peter had to point out in verse 15 that "these are not drunk as you suppose." The onlookers were "supposing" because these Spirit-filled people looked drunk. The spirit of religion will come in and point out how this just doesn't feel religious, and he's right. When the Holy Spirit comes in power, His manifestations don't feel religious—but they do bring a dimension of heaven to Earth. When the Holy Spirit first came, there was a mighty rushing, a sound from heaven, tongues of fire, and an outbreak of "utterance." It was loud, visual, and very active. We get a similar picture of the throne room of God in Revelation 4, where lightning, thundering, voices, lamps of fire, and strange creatures don't stop making noise day or night.

Paul indicated that when he showed up, it was not going to be a quiet religious time.

> I, brethren, when I came to you, did not come with excellence of speech or of wisdom declaring to you the testimony of God…

> I was with you in weakness, in fear, and in much trembling. And my speech and my preaching were not with persuasive words of human wisdom, but in demonstration of the Spirit and power, that your faith should not be in the wisdom of men but in the power of God.
>
> —1 Corinthians 2:1, 3–5

By his own account, Paul wasn't a good speaker and apparently had a fear disorder when speaking. Yet when he showed up, he brought the same Holy Spirit of Acts 2, and there was some kind of "demonstration of the Spirit and of power." For those looking for it, here's your Biblical basis for the manifestations that we see on people who experience the power of God. It doesn't say what exactly they were or what they weren't, but there was clear evidence that greater power was in the room.

The alternative to life in the Holy Spirit is described in 2 Timothy 3:

> Know this, that in the last days perilous times will come: For men will be lovers of themselves, lovers of money, boasters, proud, blasphemers, disobedient to parents, unthankful, unholy, unloving, unforgiving, slanderers, without self-control, brutal, despisers of good, traitors, headstrong, haughty, lovers of pleasure rather than lovers of God, *having a form of godliness but denying its power.* And from such a people turn away!
>
> —2 Timothy 3:1–5, emphasis added

It's interesting that this passage relates specifically to the last days when there are to be "perilous times" and people have "a form of godliness" missing its power. "For the kingdom of God is not in word but in power" (1 Cor. 4:20). Practicing a gospel without power produces a very inferior brand of Christianity whose followers look more like lovers of pleasure than lovers of God. The purpose of embracing a Spirit-centric gospel is to produce passionate lovers of God. It's very hard to be passionate about a God who no longer talks, heals, delivers, or manifests in some capacity.

Taking the mountain of religion and worship is an assignment for radical, passionate, lovesick for God, Holy Spirit-hungry Elijah revolutionaries. If all you have is platitudes and principles, stay off this mountain. Paul said it was dangerous for people to get their faith only from that. (See 1 Corinthians 2:5.) Stay off the mountain if you love meetings that start and finish like clockwork. Stay off this mountain if you like three songs and a prayer and consider that worship. Stay off this mountain if you have never had a supernatural experience with God and you still don't want one. Stay off this mountain if you like neat and tidy religion. Stay off this mountain if you like a river you can dip your toes in, but not one that will sweep you into the depths and will force you to swim. (See Ezekiel 47.)

God needs fire-branded, holy, radical men and women on this mountain, and then false religions will be displaced at an even greater pace. Don't make an idol of anything that will steal your personal passion for the Lord, and don't let the spirit of religion deceive you into stopping and camping anywhere on your walk with the Lord. You must stay "moving with the cloud," as the children of Israel had to do so that the Lord could finally get them into a Promised Land to dispossess seven nations greater and mightier than them.

WHAT THE HOLY SPIRIT INSTILLS AND INSTALLS

I have only briefly addressed some of the above functions of the Holy Spirit, but I want to emphasize that the Holy Spirit's work is not just emotionalism. It's a very comprehensive work that can leave us looking like Jesus in character and power. It is also the work of the Holy Spirit to establish the proper church structure built upon apostles and prophets, with Jesus Christ being the Chief Cornerstone. He manifests Himself in the church with:

- *God's character*—the fruit of the Holy Spirit (Galatians 5:22–23)

- *God's power*—the gifts of the Holy Spirit (1 Corinthians 12:1–11)

- *God's structure*—the five-fold ministry of the church (Ephesians 4:11–13)

LEVELS OF THE MOUNTAIN

I have already mentioned that the major religions of the world are at the top of this mountain. Christianity is already there, but the Lord is upgrading our understanding of the fullness of our inheritance. Islam, Hinduism, and Buddhism are there with us. Further down the mountain are some of the folk religions of China, Africa, and elsewhere, and then at the low levels are a multitude of cults and localized religious practices.

Behind the physical religions at the top are the invisible powers we've discussed: the spirit of religion, the Perizzites (idolatry), and the prince of Persia. These are the spirits we will need to remove. True worshippers have been given authority to displace every enemy from the top of this mountain—"so the Lord GOD will cause righteousness and praise to spring forth before all the nations" (Isa. 61:11). Ultimately the mountain of religion will be the mountain of true worship, and praise will spring forth before all nations.

THE GEOGRAPHICAL STRONGHOLD OF RELIGION

Geographically, Jerusalem sits atop of the mountain of religion. Four major religions view this as a capital of sorts. The religious spirit, aware of the latter-day role Jerusalem will play, zealously attempts to circumvent the inevitable fulfillment of prophecy. His claws must—and will—be removed from that city, and there will be a worldwide ripple effect. We know it as the place over which Jesus wept and where His blood was literally spilled, and multiple scriptures speak of natural Jerusalem's awesome destiny.

> Pray for the peace of Jerusalem; May they prosper who love you.
> —PSALM 122:6

Blessed be the LORD out of Zion, Who dwells in Jerusalem!

—PSALM 135:21

If I forget you, O Jerusalem, Let my right hand forget its skill! If I do not remember you, Let my tongue cling to the roof of my mouth—If I do not exalt Jerusalem Above my chief joy.

—PSALM 137:5–6

Like birds flying about, So will the LORD of hosts defend Jerusalem. Defending, He will also deliver it; Passing over, he will preserve it.

—ISAIAH 31:5

I have set watchmen on your walls, O Jerusalem; They shall never hold their peace day or night. You who make mention of the LORD, do not keep silent, And give Him no rest till He establishes And till He makes Jerusalem a praise in the earth.

—ISAIAH 62:6–7

Thus says the Lord: "I am returning to Jerusalem with mercy; My house shall be built in it," says the LORD of hosts, "And a surveyor's line shall be stretched out over Jerusalem."

—ZECHARIAH 1:16

The LORD will take possession of Judah as His inheritance in the Holy Land, and will again choose Jerusalem.

—ZECHARIAH 2:12

Thus says the LORD: "I will return to Zion, And dwell in the midst of Jerusalem. Jerusalem shall be called the City of Truth, the Mountain of the LORD of hosts, The Holy Mountain."

—ZECHARIAH 8:3

Jerusalem will one day be called the City of Truth. That's its inevitable destiny. It will be the Lord's mountain—His *holy* mountain.

Therefore Jerusalem itself becomes a primary battlefield to release truth on the whole mountain of religion.

WHAT THE BIBLE SAYS ABOUT RELIGION AND THE END TIMES

We have covered many scriptures, but I still want to look at two passages that deal with the end times. Isaiah 2 has been our theme chapter on the latter days when the Lord's house will be exalted. It extensively covers the last judgment on idolatry.

> Their land is also full of idols; They worship the work of their own hands, That which their own fingers have made. (verse 8)

> For the day of the LORD of hosts shall come upon everything proud and lofty; Upon everything lifted up—and it shall be brought low. (verse 12)

> The LORD alone will be exalted in that day, but the idols He shall utterly abolish…when He arises to shake the earth mightily (verses 17–19).

> In that day a man shall cast away his idols of silver and his idols of gold, Which they made, each for himself to worship, To the moles and bats. To go into the clefts of the rock, And into the crags of the rugged rocks, From the terror of the LORD and the glory of His majesty, When He arises to shake the earth mightily. (verses 20–21)

All these verses further confirm that the taking of these mountains will come with a whole lot of help from on high. The promise that Israel always had as they were told to enter into the Promised Land was that God would go before them and fight for them. Our job is just to position ourselves for the ensuing occupation of the mountain.

The other passage we need to examine is Daniel 12. This chapter full of peril, promise, and intrigue. By its own account, it's veiled and mysterious. It begins with the announcement of the archangel Michael:

> At that time Michael shall stand up, The great prince who watches over the sons of your people; And there shall be a time of trouble, Such as never was since there was a nation, Even to that time. And at that time your people shall be delivered. (verse 1)

In this very day of trouble, particularly for Israel, there is great promise for the shining sons of the kingdom.

> Those who are wise shall shine Like the brightness of the firmament, and those who turn many to righteousness Like the stars forever and ever. (verse 3)

Daniel then asks in verse 6:

> "How long shall the fulfillment of these wonders be?"

The answer comes in verse 7:

> "When the power of the holy people has been completely shattered, all these things shall be finished."

Daniel heard but did not understand.

> And he said, "Go your way Daniel, for the words are closed up and sealed till the time of the end…none of the wicked shall understand, but the wise shall understand." (verses 9–10)

This last statement is huge. It means we can expect a progressive unveiling of the secrets of Daniel 12 as we near the time of the end, which will occur "when the power of the holy people has been completely shattered." Since we see that this is a very good time for the wise, we can assume that they are not the "holy people" who will be completely shattered. I see it as a reference to a time when all other religious power is completely shattered, a time when Isaiah 2 is fulfilled and all idols and idolaters are judged.

A time is coming when the mountain of religion will become completely possessed by the bright and shining wise, and at this time all other religious power will be completely shattered. The Hebrew word is *naphats,* which means "shatter, break, dash, beat in pieces, pulverize." A complete dismantling and pulverizing of the religious spirit's operations—as well as all those who have not come out from his influence—is coming.

Our Last Religious Enemy

Islam is the only widespread religion other than Judaism and Christianity that is monotheistic. Muslims represent 20 percent of the world's population and currently dominate world attention in a largely negative way. The prince of Persia principality holds more than one billion souls in captivity. This religion carries many elements of the Antichrist in it and may in fact be a manifestation of the Antichrist. Islam is anti-Israel and anti-Christian, as well as an oppressor of women and willing to sacrifice the lives of children for their cause. These are all trademarks of the Antichrist, yet I do not see them as the final enemy of the true bride of Christ in the last days.

I see a day coming soon when the blinding power behind Islam is shattered, and all of a sudden people who were held captive can see. I see a day when Islam collapses almost in the way that communism and the iron curtain collapsed. It's already daily eroding, but a coming event will trigger a mass defection of millions of Muslims into the house of the Lord. What they will bring to the house of the Lord is something the mountain of worship really needs: the passion, zeal, and purity that they will inject into the church. They will embrace all of the supernatural inheritance that much of the church has to this point rejected. This day is coming soon and will be a part of the extreme makeover coming to the body of Christ. We will be shocked at how quickly and powerfully the crushing of Islam takes place. It is not our last religious enemy.

Our last religious enemy will be more difficult to discern: that which has come onto the mountain of religion calling itself Christian. Just as Jesus faced the greatest persecution from the very ones who were supposedly looking for the Messiah, so too will the advancing church face its greatest challenge from those who profess Jesus. These will be the final "holy people" to be completely shattered. They will not be our enemies, but we will be their enemies.

It is very possible that the ruling principality under whom they will operate will be "the prince of Greece"—the spirit of human reason. A last-days team of the religious spirit and the prince of Greece will be a huge challenge to overcome. As in Jesus day, it will be so-called holy people who theoretically are for God, but since He came in a different package than they imagined they desperately reject and fight Him. Left-brain Christianity will be the last great religious enemy that the church of Jesus Christ will have to face. This is the version of Christianity that is the form of godliness that denies its power.

The reason this form of Christianity will be such a difficult enemy is that, for a season, it will be mixed in with the advancing true church. A time is coming when it will seem as if the whole world is converting or about to convert. No other major religion will be left to knock off the mountain. At this time, the religious spirit will again reinvent himself and team up with the prince of Greece. All those believers who have not been freed from rationalism will come under its power. They will then attempt to use Christianity's newfound power to advance their version of Christianity with reason and sophistication. This last Antichrist will look good, but will be in its ultimate disguise—a true wolf in sheep's clothing. I believe that this is the fourth beast horn from Daniel 7:20—"that horn which had eyes and a mouth which spoke pompous words, whose appearance was greater than his fellows."

The prince of Greece always comes in pompous words. The philosophical world that Jesus had to break into was a world that valued high-minded, sophisticated things. It was an image-driven society that was steeped in the pride of life. Oratorical skills were highly exalted and valued. Debate and persuasion were the most respected skills. This is why Jesus, His disciples, and then Paul were such an affront to the culture. "The kingdom of God is not in word but in power" (1 Cor. 4:20).

After the great harvest that will seem to sweep virtually the whole world, an antichrist will appear who will be "greater than his fellows." The spirit of antichrist showed up in Hitler and had significant power to deceive a nation. He is manifesting again in radical Islam and holds sway over nearly a billion people. His last appearance will be his most impressive. Of him Daniel 7:21 says, "I was watching; and the same horn was making war against the saints, and prevailing against them." This most heavily disguised and final Antichrist will prevail for a season against the saints who have just experienced a tremendous world harvest.

Antichrist can also be translated "against the anointing." The Greek word *Christos* means "anointing." (It's a translation of the Hebrew word for *messiah*, which also means "anointed one.") This antichrist can ultimately be discerned by its anti-anointing stance. It will be pompous and subtly opposed to all the manifestations of the Holy Spirit's power. Believers who live their lives resisting the anointing will be become an unwitting part of the Antichrist's resistance, a tool of the anti-anointing.

The other mark of the final Antichrist will be anti-Semitism. This mark will make the Antichrist stand out more than any other. This power will have worked so convincingly that it will be able to turn world opinion against the Jews. It may even do so in the name of Jesus, thus repeating a tragic error of the Crusades and other times. Believers will protect themselves from this impressive final Antichrist by being lovers of the anointing and lovers of the promised salvation of Israel.

As you may have noticed, the seeds of that last Antichrist are already sprinkled throughout Christianity. We can actually secure a quick defeat of the last Antichrist by receiving an inoculation of the Holy Spirit's anointing now so that we quickly recognize this eloquent-talking spirit. Regardless of the Antichrist's efforts, his end is assured—an it's not good.

> Until the Ancient of Days came, and a judgment was made in favor of the saints of the Most High, and the time came for the saints to possess the kingdom.
>
> —DANIEL 7:22

The end of it all is the saints possessing the kingdom here on Earth. This is established several verses earlier: "The saints of the Most High shall receive the kingdom, and possess the kingdom forever, even forever and ever" (Dan. 7:18). The kingdom is received here on Earth. "Thy kingdom come, Thy will be done on earth" (Matt. 6:10, KJV). Scripture never tells us we'll fly away to receive the kingdom. We contend for it here, and we receive it here.

HOW LONG WILL THE ANTICHRIST PREVAIL?

> He shall speak pompous words against the Most High, Shall persecute the saints of the Most High, And shall intend to change times and law. Then the saints shall be given into his hand For a time and times and half a time.
>
> —DANIEL 7:25

Though there are several speculations as to what "a time and times and half a time" means, I believe the vagueness of the timetable is in itself a notice that it is negotiable. I believe that the final refining fire that the Lord will allow upon the church will be to rid us of the prince of Greece impurities that have infiltrated into the church since Jesus' day. The other test will be whether we stand with Israel when our very life is endangered. The timetable for that purifying work is undetermined. The more unprepared we are ahead of time, the more intense the fire will be. If the Elijah Revolution fulfills its assignment, the time could be short. We could see a very quick fulfillment of the next two verses of Daniel 7.

> But the court shall be seated. And they shall take away his dominion, To consume and destroy it forever. Then the kingdom and dominion, And the greatness of the kingdom under the whole heaven, Shall be given to the people, the saints of the Most High. His kingdom is an everlasting kingdom, And all dominions shall serve and obey Him.
>
> —DANIEL 7:26–27

Notice that all of this is still taking place under heaven. That dominion is given to the saints. The Antichrist is ultimately the Lord's tool for final cleansing of His people. His bride will be "a glorious church, not having spot or wrinkle or any such thing" (Eph. 5:27).

If it surprises you that Greek thinking would be the final thing God needs to purge from His bride, then take it to heart. This is the same kind of thinking that brought Lucifer down—high-minded, image-conscious, and full of great, pompous words. He was subtle, saying only that he would be "like the Most High" (Isa. 14:14). When we think we can do something without the Holy Spirit (and His anointing), we are under the influence of that spirit of pride. The God who began a good work in us must finish it. He is Alpha and Omega. In Him—and Him alone—"we live and move and have our being" (Acts 17:28).

Resorting to our own enlightened words and deeds developed from a mind of reason may not seem like a high crime, but it caused Abraham to begat Ishmael, who still wars against the descendants of Isaac. It prevented Samuel, like David's father and brothers, from seeing David as king. It's why the seekers of the Messiah, the prophecy experts and Pharisees, could not see who the Messiah was. The very ones who allegedly sought the Anointed One were the Antichrist of the day who eventually killed Him. This set up the redemption of all humanity, as the Antichrist *greatly* overplayed his hand. But the Pharisees opposed Jesus because of the way they reasoned in their minds. (See Mark 2:6–8 for one example among many of how human reasoning opposed Jesus.)

A final prophetic passage out of Zechariah 9 tells of the final victory of the sons of Zion versus the sons of Greece. This refers to the last displacement of the holy ones that will take place on this mountain of religion/worship.

> For I have bent Judah, My bow, fitted the bow with Ephraim, And raised up your sons, O Zion, Against your sons, O Greece, And made you like the sword of a mighty man." Then the LORD will be seen over them; And His arrow will go forth like lightning, The Lord GOD will blow the trumpet, And go with the whirlwinds from the south. The LORD of hosts will defend them;

They shall devour and subdue with slingstones. They shall drink and roar as with wine; They shall be filled with blood like basins, Like the corners of the altar. The LORD their God will save them in that day, As the flock of His people. For they shall be like the jewels of a crown, Lifted like a banner over His land—For how great is His goodness, And how great its beauty! Grain shall make the young men thrive, And new wine the young women.

—ZECHARIAH 9:13–17

THE MULTI-PRONGED APPROACH

Like all other mountains, the mountain of religion requires a multi-pronged attack. The religious spirit and the Perizzites (symbolic of idolatry) on the mountain are just manifestations of false worship. All who will penetrate this mountain must have a commitment to be true worshipers. (See John 4:23.) However someone is led to invade this mountain, it must be on the back of true worship. There is no authority to displace false worship from this mountain if one is not a worshiper "in spirit and in truth" (John 4:24). In the Zechariah passage quoted above, it is Judah that the Lord bends against the "sons of Greece." The name Judah means "praise" and was the tribe that always led Israel into battle. No battle on this mountain will be won without Judah leading the way.

Worship in spirit and in truth is passionate, abandoned, radical worship. It is not three hymns and a prayer. It is not the kind of worship we can perform without having moved a muscle. True worship exalts the Lord with our bodies. We clap, dance, move, raise hands, spin, sway, tap, sweat, get tired, smile, laugh, cry, pour out emotions, and expend energy because we are entering the court of the King of the universe, and we are moved by that fact. It is the very Spirit from His presence that stirs in us to offer a sacrifice of praise. (See Jeremiah 33:11.)

Part of breaking the stronghold of Greece off of us is performed in worship. Greek thinking says, "Well, I'm worshiping in my heart." That concept of worship didn't exist in the Hebrew mindset. *All* praise and worship was participatory and active. The Greek approach to worship is like a husband telling his wife, "I thought about giving you a dozen roses today," and expecting some sort of credit for the thought. That lacks enough involvement to be considered spirit and truth. If the wife replied to her husband, "Well, I thought of cooking your favorite meal today," it would ring just as hollow. Worship *can* take place in our thoughts, but it must be much more than that if it's going to qualify as true worship.

Freedom in worship and an increase in the Holy Spirit anointing are a direct cause-and-effect that cannot be ignored. To the degree that worship lines up honestly with the rest of our daily walk with the Lord, to that same degree it becomes even more powerful. In some capacity, everything we do can express worship at some level, but intentionally lifting our hearts to the Lord in song and dance is a manifestation of true worship. It's a right-brain operation that serves to strengthen the part of us that's open to the things of God.

THE PRAYER STRATEGY

The role of intercessors on this mountain is extremely important. Prayer for Jerusalem and in Jerusalem is a priority for those who feel called to intercede for the mountain of religion. We are to pray for the peace of Jerusalem (see Psalm 122:6), but we also need to better understand how that will happen and begin to agree in prayer over the steps that lead to the peace of Jerusalem. False religions there must be eradicated.

Israel itself is being conditioned to receive the Messiah it has rejected, but there will be trouble there before peace comes. Since the presence of false gods and idols in Jerusalem is anti-peace, we must pray for the destruction and removal of the religious spirit and the Perizzites. Otherwise, we'll end up with a band-aid on a tumor that needs radical surgery.

If you are called as an intercessor for this mountain, I believe you're also called either to move to Jerusalem or spend significant time there. The roots of all religious trees find their way into that city. Prayer that takes place there affects global issues related to the mountain of religion.

The Lord will be sending increasing numbers of mighty prayer warriors and will begin to break down false religions. People who actually go to the geographical location will penetrate that mountain.

THE ACTION STRATEGY

Much of the action strategy overlaps with the prayer strategy, as a combination of the two is most powerful. There are infinite action strategies that the Lord could raise up, such as the creation of a Christian curriculum that gets widespread acceptance in school systems. One key strategy will be to discern and detect altars of world religions that need to be overthrown. Gideon, for example, started with the overthrow of his father's altar of Baal, and something was released in the spirit that caused thousands to join him. Anything is viable if it's bathed and birthed in prayer and comes as direction from the Lord.

When it all comes together in its proper fashion, the presence of apostles and prophets will be part of every strategy. For our purposes, it might be better to call them seasoned men and women of God, as the apostle and prophet titles are a dime a dozen. All true apostles will also be intercessors, so that's one way to distinguish them from non-apostles. Most premature apostles are high on strategy and not so high on prayer. They have not been broken enough to properly *under*estimate their natural efforts and strategies. Any true apostle will value his prayer life far more than he values his strategy life. An apostle's intercession doesn't necessarily need to take hours or involve travailing prayer; it's usually a detonator anointing in prayer or declaration. The bottom line is we need the function of apostles and prophets. We need the actual power and authority of these ministries to be manifested. The titles themselves can at best be a distraction and at worst be an impediment. It's more important for God and heaven to know who we are than for people to know who we are. At some point, it will be valuable for us to know who true apostles are, but that will happen when true prophets are in their place. Until then (and even then), personal discernment is a must, with the standard set by what we see in Scripture.

Hivites and the
Mountain of Celebration

B ILL BRIGHT WAS shown this mountain as the mountain of celebration. It's not as easy to identify with that name as it is with the names of other mountains, but this is the best term because this mountain encompasses so many areas of life.

WHAT IS THE MOUNTAIN OF CELEBRATION?

The mountain of celebration includes the arts, music, sports, fashion, entertainment, and every other way we celebrate and enjoy life. This mountain has so thoroughly been captured by Satan's hordes that most believers aren't sure it can even be possessed. Some, in my experience, aren't even sure this mountain *should* be taken. In the same way they view the media, they say it's all of the devil and has nothing to do with saving souls. But it can and will be taken. It must be taken because this is the mountain that captures the hearts of our youth. For several years of their lives, this is almost the only mountain that they care about, and from his position at the top, the enemy has been able to corrupt and thwart the destiny of entire generations.

Each mountain seems to be of the utmost importance. This one is no exception. This is where creativity shows up, and creativity is extremely important to God. He is initially introduced to us in Genesis 1 as Creator. His essence is creative. Satan can't do that; he can only counterfeit what has already been created. What looks like dark creativity is just a corruption or a prostitution of something God originally created to be good. Every sexual deviance Satan has come up with, for example, is his attempt to sabotage the very good, original gift God gave us. When we don't see that, we begin to reject God's good gifts because we only know the distortions of them. We are much poorer for it—that's like getting rid of one hundred dollar bills because there are so many counterfeits. That does nothing to eliminate counterfeits; it only causes us to miss what God has given us.

WHO RULES ON THIS MOUNTAIN?

The nation from Deuteronomy 7 that corresponds to the mountain of celebration is the Hivites. Their name means "villagers" and "life-giving place." These are the enemy villagers who are occupying a life-giving place. They represent counterfeit and perversion. The word *counterfeit* means "made in imitation with intent to deceive." *Perversion* means "a misinterpretation" or "to lead into a less excellent state."

The first Hivite we see in Scripture is in Genesis 34:

> Now Dinah the daughter of Leah, whom she had borne to Jacob, went out to see the daughters of the land. And when Shechem the son of Hamor the Hivite, prince of the country, saw her, he took her and lay with her, and violated her.
>
> —GENESIS 34:1–2

Our first encounter with a Hivite is a rape. When a daughter of Israel strayed in order to see the daughters of the land, a Hivite violated her purity. Shechem was then willing to do whatever it took to keep her, even agreeing to be circumcised. That is the counterfeit—an imitation with the intent to deceive. Simeon and Levi, her natural full brothers, avenged her by killing Shechem and all the men of his land. Like Shechem, a Hivite spirit is out to deceive you with a counterfeit and pervert that which is right.

The Hivites show up again in Joshua 9. The Gibeonites were Hivites, and they caused Joshua to make a treaty not to kill them by pretending to be someone they weren't.

> When the inhabitants of Gibeon heard what Joshua had done to
> Jericho and Ai, they worked craftily, and went and pretended to
> be ambassadors.
>
> —JOSHUA 9:3–4

In verse 22, Joshua accused the Gibeonites of having beguiled him. The word *beguile* in Hebrew is *ramah,* and it means "to deceive, mislead, or trick." The Hivites were able to infiltrate Israel and to use pretense and deception to keep from being destroyed.

Another interesting fact about the Hivites is that they dwelt in Mount Lebanon (Judges 3:3). Lebanon was associated with wealth—that was where the famous cedars of Lebanon came from that Solomon used to build the temple. As Israel took their Promised Land, that mountain was a possession of Benjamin, and Gibeon was Benjamin's levitical city. The insights from this are amazing: the Hivites were in a land that belonged to Levi, the priestly tribe; and the material from that land was a key part of the temple that housed the glory of God.

The enemy on this mountain of celebration is the Hivite. That's who perverts or misinterprets what is supposed to be a blessing. Even as with the account of the rape of Dinah, there is a strong sexual element to a Hivite. He takes a good thing, sex, and perverts it. He violates standards and has no moral compass. Deception and counterfeiting are his game.

The Hivites occupy Mount Lebanon. The cedars of Lebanon could represent the music, art, drama, poetry that is supposed to fill God's house and both receive and express the glory of God. The Hivites work to counterfeit, distort, and corrupt so that the cedars become warped and perverted and are then rejected by the people of God who think they are evil.

WHO IS KING OF THE HIVITES?

The principality on this mountain of celebration is *Jezebel.* The name means "unchaste," or "Baal is husband." Baal, of course, was the god of the land that was constantly leading Israel astray. It was the principal god of Tyre—a very wealthy city in the Hivite region of Mount

Lebanon. Jezebel uses a good gift from God, sex, and perverts it by abusing God's rules for it. Someone who is unchaste has actually used this gift but has misinterpreted the purpose of it.

We associate Jezebel with seduction and lust, and that fits the profile. Seduction is a misinterpretation of romance, and lust is a misinterpretation of love. Jezebel has been a dominant power over the United States, as well over the church itself. When it teams up with the religious spirit, it is particularly insidious. Jezebel works to sabotage all the pleasures of God.

> You will show me the path of life; In Your presence is fullness of
> joy; At Your right hand are pleasures forevermore.
> —PSALM 16:11

God is a God of pleasure and joy. Joy is a foundational makeup of His kingdom. (See Romans 14:17.) He is the Creator of sex, music, art, poetry, drama, and every beautiful and enjoyable thing. These gifts are the part of His glory that already fills the earth. Jezebel counterfeits and perverts them so that we are either violated (defiled) or we try to live out our Christian life with no pleasure and joy—which explains why there are so many dour and serious Christians. At God's right hand are pleasures for evermore, and Jezebel seeks to prostitute that pleasure by enticing us to be "lovers of pleasures more than lovers of God" (2 Timothy 3:4). What is good in the right measure is then sin when indulged in too much or improperly. Homosexuality, bisexuality, bestiality, adultery, fornication, pornography, prostitution, and pedophilia are all Jezebel's misinterpretations of one of God's greatest gifts.

Likewise, music is clearly a gift of God that expresses the profound hunger of our spirit, even beyond our ability to understand it. This amazing gift has been so perverted by Jezebel that we are left without much of a grid for even determining which music is good and which is bad. One version comes from the Hivites' misinterpretation, and the other is from God. We will look for clues and guidelines for extracting the good from the bad in music and other forms of celebration.

The Important Role of the Prophet

The role of prophets and the prophetic is huge, a very important key in displacing Jezebel and her Hivites and taking this mountain. Part of this should be very obvious to us. It was the prophet Elijah, in fact, who was Jezebel's avowed enemy. His confrontation with her eventually led to her downfall.

A specific and primary target of the Elijah Revolution is to take the mountain that is presently releasing a dark and decadent pop culture. God will release the Elijah Revolution tsunami onto this mountain, and when it is taken, every form of entertainment and celebration will prophesy of God. Music, art, poetry, fashion, and film are all meant to prophesy to a culture. They are supposed to be ever-changing and always advancing, because God is always on the move. We cannot prophesy with five hundred-year-old hymns, with one-hundred-year-old fashions, or with any other art that doesn't carry something fresh and revelatory about God. A distinguishing characteristic of anything that proceeds from God is that it is not stale and boring. As we keep moving with God, He continues to reveal and release fresh and creative sounds, pictures, and styles that the world can ultimately only be in awe of. On a scale of one to ten, the arts and music we have modeled so far before the world is about a two. Jezebel meanwhile, continues to prophesy to an entire generation through her own dark and lustful counterfeits.

We know from the book of Revelation that Jezebel was not just a person who lived in Elijah's day. She is referred to as a demonic power:

> Nevertheless I have a few things against you, because you allow that woman Jezebel, who calls herself a prophetess, to teach and seduce My servants.
>
> —REVELATION 2:20

We don't know if Jezebel is just another face of Satan himself or an actual assistant contractor of hell. Regardless, this spirit must be—and *will* be—dispossessed from this mountain.

MUSIC THAT PROPHESIES

One of the definitions of prophesying in the original Hebrew is "to sing." We know prophets would call for musicians to play (2 Kings 3:15)—it would stimulate the *naba,* or "bubbling forth" (another one of the words for prophecy in the Old Testament). Sometimes the song itself was a prophecy, or the prophecy could be "bubbled forth" by a musician. Beside these factors, the scripture shows us yet another prophetic connection to music and their ability to prophesy.

> Moreover David and the captains of the army separated for the service some of the sons of Asaph…who should prophesy with harps, stringed instruments, and cymbals.
>
> —1 CHRONICLES 25:1

Not only can a singing voice prophesy, and not only does music stir the prophetic, but even instruments can prophesy. An instrument can bubble forth with a sound of heaven that releases a dimension of heaven here on Earth. We see that during the dedication of Solomon's temple in 2 Chronicles 5.

> And it came to pass when the priests came out of the Most Holy Place…and the Levites who were the singers…stood at the east end of the altar, clothed in white linen, having cymbals, stringed instruments and harps, and with them one hundred and twenty priests sounding with trumpets—indeed it came to pass, when the trumpets and the singers were as one, to make one sound to be heard in praising and thanking the LORD, and when they lifted up their voice with the trumpets and cymbals and instruments of music, and praised the LORD saying; "For He is good, For His mercy endures forever," that the house, the house of the LORD, was filled with a cloud, so that the priests could not continue ministering because of the cloud; for the glory of the LORD filled the house of God.
>
> —2 CHRONICLES 5:11–14

When all the prophetic instruments of voices, music, and instruments were united, the glory of the Lord descended and the musicians were overtaken by the glory. This is the power of music when it's in the hands of God's children. It can bring the glory of the Lord to earth—a literal, physical presence that overtakes those in the flow of it. This particular instance of the glory descending was not in the course of a normal meeting but during the celebration of the temple being finished. We are now, though rarely, accessing the glory of God that is available for us as we bring our prophetic instruments of the arts under the "bubbling forth" of the Spirit of God.

This, of course, is why Satan wants to pervert and misinterpret music and worship. He can give lesser demonic or soulish highs through the counterfeit being released. Angry highs, lustful highs, sad highs, false hope highs, and revenge highs can all be released through a gift of God (music) that is perverted and counterfeited. Ultimately the world needs music in order to feel something. The only thing worse than a counterfeit feeling is *no* feeling. One way or another, people will search for some kind of music that will touch something, anything other than the blandness of life without Christ.

WHAT ABOUT CHRISTIAN MUSIC ARTISTS?

While many of us have some kind of understanding that a worship service can bring some of the presence of the Lord, we may not know what to think of the performances of Christian music artists. Is this industry even acceptable to God, or is it a virtual prostitution of God's gift?

I believe that the Christian music industry is perilously close to a slippery ledge that slides into Jezebel's camp. On one hand, having its headquarters in Nashville puts it in a great position to displace the enemy, who produces its counterfeits there. On the other hand, however, being in Nashville sets up its camp awfully close to a darker influence. The difference is in whether Christian artists are the influencers or the influencees. One is a vital role; the other is very dangerous.

Like Dinah, many artists are straying out "to see the daughters of the land." That can set them up for defilement. If we have this powerful gift of the Lord, we cannot produce music the Hivite way. Something must be different; otherwise we end up with a Hivite product with Christian lyrics—a distant second on the desirability chart for teens or others to hear.

I do believe that having Christian artists in the music industry can be a good thing. Any alternative to Jezebel that fills the airwaves is valuable. By and large, however, our musicians seem to rarely access the awesome, raw, creativity of our God, but rather follow the world's cues about what is hip, cool, and cutting edge. This means that the same influences behind Jezebel's music are allowed to influence ours— as though Jezebel could come up with a better product than the God who created music. Even when we do have a decent product, we tend to make a deal with the Hivites. For many artists, it's more important to receive honor from the world than to hear the approval of God.

The central problem is that most believers who have had a significant artistic gift have never had a real understanding of the kingdom of God and what we are called to do. God is releasing this Elijah Revolution so there will be understanding of our assignment and our authority. Acts 2:7 repeats Joel's prophesy that says that "in the last days I [God] will pour out of My Spirit on all flesh…and Your sons and Your daughters will prophesy." A holy invasion of Elijah revolutionaries who know who they are and understand their assignment is coming upon this mountain. They will not be talked into compromise with the Hivites or with Jezebel. They will ascend this mountain on a mission to displace every distortion and counterfeit of God's great gifts of pleasure that He means for us to have even on Earth. There will be such great grace upon these revolutionaries that they will be exalted even in the eyes of the world. New sounds and rhythms from God's house and His people will be broadcast over the airwaves of the nations, and the world will know that this music is special.

When that happens, secular artists will begin to take their cues from the kingdom of God as it manifests through His children. They will add *their* lyrics to *our* music, rather than the other way around, as it has been for much too long. And even with the wrong lyrics, something of heaven will be released over the airwaves. Truly we will see the sons and daughters of God take the top of the hill of music that's on the mountain of celebration.

How Important Is Skill?

As we discuss the various arts on the mountain of celebration, we will need to address the question of skill. Our local church has talked about this a lot as we've tried to come up with a balance. We don't want to prioritize skill over anointing, but we also understand that if someone is really anointed in an area, then some level of skill should either be there or be readily attainable. We don't want lazy anointed musicians and singers; neither do we want musicians and singers who are skilled but lack the character or spirit required.

Earlier in this chapter, we looked at 1 Chronicles 25:1—the passage where David appointed some of the sons of Asaph to prophesy musically. That passage goes on to address the matter of skill, "So the number of them, with their brethren who were instructed in the songs of the LORD, all who were skillful was two hundred and eighty-eight" (verse 7). Consider also what David wrote in Psalm 33:

> Rejoice in the Lord, O you righteous! For praise from the upright
> is beautiful. Praise the Lord with the harp; Make melody to Him
> with an instrument of ten strings. Sing to Him a new song; Play
> skillfully with a shout of joy.
>
> —PSALM 33:1–3

There are other passages that let us know how important skill was during the reigns of David and Solomon. This verse is insightful in that he wanted a "new song." Prophetic music is always a new song, the bubbling forth from a prophetic flow that can surface when we are in a deep place of worship with God.

If we overestimate the value of skill and make it an idol, however, we can fill a worship team or a Christian band with natural excellence that's empty of the spirit of excellence. The Levites of 2 Chronicles 5:11 were first described as those who came "out of the Most Holy Place" before they were listed as skillful. The "holy place" is the first priority.

The level of skill must not be detrimental to a good sound, but we will get a distortion of what God wants if we prioritize the wrong thing.

The goal is to have skill, anointing, and passion—and an abundance of all three. The greater the exposure God is giving us, the more we must be advancing in all three. If one is low, there should be more of the others. Even the world values passion and will overlook certain technical faults if the overall product is good. (Their other value is sex appeal, which comes from the Jezebel influence they are under.)

We need to be clear on this: skill alone will never convince the world that we are plugged into a greater creative flow. Excellence will not, by itself, win or prove anything. We are looking for an "it" factor that is unexplainable and divine. This factor is the favor and anointing of God that may defy natural perceptions. It's the fingerprint of God on us that tells the world, "Hey, you need to listen to this." This is what caused the people to realize these uneducated, ordinary disciples had been with Jesus. (See Acts 4:13.) It is also the stature and favor that Jesus had: "And Jesus increased in wisdom and stature and in favor with God and men" (Luke 2:52).

If Christians are to be the lead domino in the world of music—or any area of celebration and culture—we must have people who know their kingdom identity. This identity is the purpose or mission of taking this mountain of celebration/arts and displacing the enemy off of it. If we know the specific enemy is Jezebel and her counterfeiting, perverting Hivites, we can climb this mountain wearing the appropriate armor. May an uncompromising army arise and begin to move forward on this mountain.

ART THAT PROPHESIES

The art of one world-class artist is selling for between fifty thousand and one million dollars per piece. Akiane is twelve years old and has been on every imaginable television show and drawn unbelievable secular attention. Yet she is a very devoted, uncompromising Christian, who freely confesses that her art depicts heaven, which she has visited several times since she was four. No one can really argue with her because her art is so profound and awe-inspiring that it clearly has that "been with

Jesus" fingerprint on it. She is a perfect first-fruit example of what will be coming out of the house of the Lord.

Akiane's excellence is impressive, but it is what she has seen that makes her art such a great treasure. She has said that when she teaches children how to draw, she is actually teaching them how to see. She may not even know it, but she is functioning out of a powerful prophetic gifting.

The awesome power of God contained in His creative release is available for His kids. We can try for hours to tell someone just how compassionate and kind He is, but Akiane has a picture of His face and eyes that speaks more than a thousand words could.

An invasion of Elijah Revolution kids (of any age) is about to take the world by storm. The art will be excellent, but what they have seen will be what really captures the world's imagination, and that will begin to bring down a measure of heaven to earth. In all the arts, as we on earth agree with heaven, we release heaven on earth. There are sounds of heaven to be captured that will cause the world to buckle to its knees and confess that there is a God. There are images of heaven that will convince the world of the reality of His supernatural dimension. Art actually releases into the atmosphere whatever is captured on its easel. Redemption, forgiveness, rejoicing, mercy, hope, faith, and love can all be released through art. This powerful tool must be fully recovered as a weapon by the children of God of this generation.

MOVIES THAT PROPHESY

All movies have a prophetic power to them. Jezebel uses them to release her darkness and decadence. *Brokeback Mountain* released permission for homosexual behavior across the globe. The Harry Potter movies released acceptance of the occult. These are only two examples among many.

We have only recently begun to see some godly prophesying come out of Hollywood. *The Passion of Christ* was huge in its global impact, and we will only fully know how great it was in eternity. It was important that God show the world how severe of a price He paid for the earth before He begins to manifest Himself as Lord of hosts and Ruler of the nations. We tend to look at the impact of these things in terms of the number of conversions, but there's much more to it than that. This movie served as a John the Baptist-type precursor to Jesus' lordship on Earth. God's righteous judgments come on the heels of establishing His right to this planet and every one on it. The whole world was left with an image of Jesus and the cross and a higher level of accountability.

The *Lord of the Rings* trilogy also released prophetic announcements and warnings to the world, though with less biblical theology than *The Passion*. Ending with *The Return of the King* was one way the Lord got a measure of His message out. So was *The Chronicles of Narnia,* a movie that clearly laid out Jesus' work on the cross and showed Him as a returning Lion. These are very powerful not just as evangelism but as a prophetic "preparing of the way" before the Lord's new level of intervention in the affairs of men. Jesus said that if His people don't get the right message and response out, God would raise up stones to cry out (Luke 19:40). Rocks may or may not get all the theology just right, but they can serve God's purposes.

So the Lord is going to raise and release a new kind of prophet, one that prophesies through movies, television shows, or Broadway productions. These Hollywood prophets will understand the kingdom of God and the mountain from which Jezebel must be displaced. The goal will not just be having Christian fare on television or at the theater; that's a weak and flimsy compromise, not a revolution. It's not enough just to portray Sunday school on the big screens and expect that to displace Hollywood's products. In the heart of our Creator are the most exciting stories and adventures in the world—and they aren't fiction, though they can be portrayed as such. Prophets will see something in the Spirit that will capture the hearts and minds of a generation and use entertainment media to prophesy it. These revolutionaries are going to see into God's heart and be the new Elijahs of our generation.

SPORTS THAT PROPHESY

As Indianapolis Colts head coach Tony Dungy raised the Super Bowl trophy in 2007, he acknowledged that though he was glad to be the first African-American coach to win a Super Bowl, he was more satisfied with something else: that he and Bears coach Lovie Smith were both Christians who were glad to be able to model that the Lord's ways work, even in football.

Much had been said and written about how different the coaching philosophy of these men was from previous models of coaching success. A good coach was someone who would cuss his players out, yell at them, get in their face, and through intense schemes, motivate his men to perform their best. Tony started the practice season by telling his players in an even, normal voice: "Men, pay attention because this is as loud as I'm going to get all year." Not only did these men model fruit of the spirit coaching, but Tony had to go through the very public suicide of his son the previous year. The testimony of his life, combined with his coaching style, made him a much greater ambassador for the kingdom of God than a host of TV preachers could. He displayed godliness, and God gave him a platform to prophesy. Better yet, Tony didn't miss his opportunity to testify that there's even a godly way to coach pro football.

All believers with sports platforms have a ministry. Most haven't recognized it, and most of those who have recognized it only see the opportunity as a platform for the gospel of salvation. If athletes are only able to say, "I, too, have made a decision for Jesus," they miss the point. A champion boxer once was very vocal about being a Christian, even while he was having multiple affairs and marriages. No one on these mountains does any good by only talking of salvation. What we need is those who will model the Lord's way, who understand that we must demonstrate a reality that far exceeds talk. I don't believe that this boxer failed just because he had moral issues. He failed because he didn't really know his godly assignment.

Our assignment is to demonstrate God's kingdom as a different way of doing things. Jezebel must be displaced from this mountain of celebration. That boxer's life revealed that he was trying to love God while yielding to Jezebel, and that mixture just won't work. This man's presence on the mountain was counterproductive to the advancement of the kingdom of God.

Tony Dungy and Lovie Smith serve as prophetic evidence of the principle of this book—that God is releasing a tsunami that is intended to lift God's people to the tops of the mountains. They are part of the latter day of Isaiah 2:2 when Lord's house will be exalted above all other mountains. They are spiritual pioneers with a breaker anointing to release an entirely new model of coaching to the world. Christian men of character who are also good coaches will now be in a higher demand than ranting, cussin' coaches of the past.

If you are a Christian of influence who is involved in sports, know that you are raised up and blessed by God to be a prophetic voice in and to your generation. You are not called to say, "I keep my religion private"—that would make you a salt-shaker with no salt, a Christian with no kingdom value. It is incumbent on you to see that you've been placed on the mountain of celebration with an advancing kingdom purpose. If you don't see that, you have almost no hope of sustaining resistance against Jezebel. You must be taken over by the fire of the spirit of Elijah, or Jezebel will take you out. This is your ministry, your platform, your pulpit—*not* your secular life.

Fashion That Prophesies

If you believe that fashion is of the devil…well, you may be right. If you are, however, it's only because we have *given* it to the devil. Fashion is another prophetic tool, and if we don't engage this part of the mountain, the world will continue to prophesy with fashion.

That this industry has been under Jezebel's jurisdiction is obvious by the sexualized styles that are prevalent. Some fashion designs very obviously carry Jezebel on them, while others may manifest a lesser amount. A high proportion of fashion designers and trendsetters are homosexual. If a clothing style draws sexual attention as its first calling card, we can be sure that we are seeing Jezebel at work.

Jezebel is at the top of this mountain to release two things—lust and death. That's her influence, whether in movies, music, or fashion. If she can combine all three, she is even more effective. For example, in the nineties a music style and an accompanying fashion came out of Seattle, Washington. Kurt Cobain became the primary "prophet" for what came to be known as grunge culture as it was released worldwide and still carries repercussions today. Cobain was a musician who helped reshape popular music, and the music released a corresponding fashion.

Cobain was a young man profoundly affected by the divorce of his parents. He had lifetime battles with depression, chronic bronchitis, and severe stomach pain that no one was able to properly diagnose. His music captured a raw, passionate cry of pain and despair that resonated with a generation. He died in 1994 from a self-inflicted shotgun wound to the head.[1]

The grunge culture screamed, "I hate myself." Both the music and the fashion carried hopelessness and a spirit of suicide. Its appeal was in reaching down and touching a very real pain, but it only left people raw. It was authentic, but only in its diagnosis of hurts. There was no remedy for the despair, only identification with it. This pain was the ache of a fatherless generation, of family breakdown, and of fathers failing to be fathers—of Generation X being abandoned by parents in full-throttle pursuit of the American dream.

The Goth subculture is also an example of music combined with style. This fashion style promotes death and gloom and is very widespread. Dark attire and makeup that come from the influence of Jezebel are its most visible marks. It prophesies death, depression, hopelessness, and suicide. Some well-meaning believers have embraced the look in order to reach the culture, but that's an ill-conceived strategy. It's an alliance with the Hivites that will bear very little long-term fruit. Some kids don't mean any harm by dressing Goth, but they don't realize how they are yielding themselves to prophesy a message of death with their fashion.

Fashion has also given us the heroine chic look that functions to prophesy Jezebel's message of addiction. One constant throughout recent fashion history is Jezebel's ability to flaunt and model seductive styles. Believers should not wear these styles because they're prophetic messages.

The point is not for us to wear conservative clothing but to come up with radical styles that release the kingdom of God on Earth. To this point, WWJD bracelets are the closest thing we've seen of a Christian fashion trend. Even multitudes of non-believers thought it was cool to wear those bracelets. But we're going further than that. Some Elijah revolutionaries are going to get a hold of this idea and begin to prophesy with a fashion style that captivates the world.

If you are a believer who loves fashion, ask God if He has put you here to be a unique kind of prophet for the advancement of the kingdom. You'll need to recognize the world's influences from Jezebel and avoid mixing them in with what God inspires you to create. In His creative heart, He knows what fashions can capture the hearts of a generation. He just needs someone to see it and then reproduce it.

It only takes a spark to start a fire. Know who you are. Know what mountain you are called to. Know who your enemy is. Know your mission—and then be released.

LEVELS OF THE MOUNTAIN

The mountain of celebration affects and even creates pop culture. Those whose platform reaches millions are at the top of this mountain. I haven't covered other sources of entertainment, but they seem to be much lower down the mountain. Our specific call is to take the top of the mountain and displace powers and principalities at that level. This affects the second heaven thought life of cities, regions, and nations. If you are already positioned in a place of some influence that's lower on the mountain, then go ahead and secure that area for the kingdom of God. You are an ambassador, you are in ministry (as we all are), and as you are lit up with the fire of the spirit of Elijah, you can begin to release heaven all around you.

Geographically, Hollywood is clearly at the top of the mountain. New York, Seattle, Las Vegas, San Francisco, and New Orleans also have altars close to the top of the mountain. If these geographical locations are not secured in the Spirit by the sons and daughters of the King, they will receive very severe judgments. For New Orleans (the center of Mardi Gras and voodoo), hurricane Katrina was an example. San Francisco has a sentence of judgment hanging over it, tied into it being the homosexual hub of the nation and maybe the world. Righteous judgments will assist us in retaking these geographical areas. The judgment will be a platform from which to call out for repentance.

Many people have a problem with the idea of God releasing or allowing catastrophic judgments on cities, but He does. They are an extension of His great grace. If He sees a city heading into hell, He will intervene and overturn the boat, even if lives are lost. Why? Because some could turn back and be spared. If they proceed to get back on the boat, He'll knock them over again in an attempt to save them before a final harsh judgment. When severe judgment saves someone from an even worse judgment, it's an act of grace.

Some cities are known for forms of entertainment that shouldn't even be saved. Las Vegas gambling, for example, has no redemptive value. There is not a Christian gambling alternative, just as there are no Christian prostitution alternatives or Christian strip clubs. Some entertainment is fit only for elimination.

The Lord has His sons and daughters working in all the cities mentioned above to bring His redemption to bear in those places. Wherever Satan comes in like a flood, there the Lord will raise a standard. He will work on behalf of His active ambassadors in all places of darkness. Each city has the potential to turn around and become the spearhead of a special move of God. History itself tells us that. The Azusa Street Revival proceeded from Los Angeles beginning in April of 1906. On September 23, 1857, Jeremy Lanphier rented a hall on Fulton Street in New York City and began a prayer movement that led to what some call the Third Great Awakening. Only six people came the first day for the lunch prayer time, and there was a slow, gradual increase—until the stock market crashed a few days later. Within six months the prayer movement had spread around the nation, and more than ten thousand were meeting every noon in New York City alone. It eventually jumped to other nations, too.

God's shaking of cities and nations works hand-in-hand with His people doing their part to bring about a kingdom revolution. Four days after the Asuza Street Revival began, San Francisco experienced the infamous Great San Francisco Earthquake of 1906 that devastated the city. In New York, it was less than three weeks after Jeremy Lanphier began his prayer meetings that the stock market crashed. God's shaking assists His initiatives that are being activated by His children. At some point, however, a city can be so given over to sin that the Lord will instruct His children to leave that city before He sends catastrophic judgment there.

A Multi-Pronged Approach

There are cities to be strategically targeted. There are institutions to be targeted. There are individuals to be targeted. There are altars to overthrow and many things to displace. But we must always remember to come in with a replacement for what was formerly there. Satan returns seven times stronger if we only knock him off the mountain with out replacing him.

The Hollywood ratings board is a very important target, as are Disney and Motown. The critics who write reviews and committees that give awards like the Oscars and Grammys are also extremely important—their seal of approval can jumpstart movies and musicians who have no business being jumpstarted. The most important directive or strategy, however, is hearing from the Lord. It's possible to waste a lot of time going after something that seems strategic when, if we just allowed the Lord to promote us, mountains would crumble around us. The taking of this mountain is a spiritual war, and we must never lose sight of that reality. Ultimately what will cause the collapse of every mountain of the enemy is the Lord's house being exalted in a specific arena. His celebration will begin to release disfavor and decimation on the enemy's celebrations.

ARE WORSHIPERS ON THIS MOUNTAIN
OR ON THE RELIGION MOUNTAIN?

If you are a worship leader you may be asking if your mountain is the religion mountain or the celebration mountain. The answer is that it can be both. It is very possible to move across several of these mountains at the same time, particularly if one receives great favor. Worship itself shows up on both of these mountains. That was the case for Old Testament Israel. Daily, regular worship took place on the mountain of religion. But then there was also the celebration of the feasts several times a year (Passover or Pentecost), as well as special-occasion dedicatory celebrations (Solomon's temple). These celebrations were not times of fundamental discipleship regularly occurring in religious life. They were exciting, special occasions—good times that people looked forward to. Yet worshippers were very instrumental in both.

In a modern-day church context, mountain of religion celebration would be leading worship in regular church services, and mountain of celebration worship would be more like what we do at large conference gatherings. We have much growing to do with regard to the latter. In the future, we will have celebration conferences where every form of godly creativity will be on display. These events—essentially Christian arts festivals—will showcase all the awesome creativity of God through His people. They will not carry the second-rate creativity we've often been known for in the past. They will showcase the best art, the best music, the best food, the best dramas, the best poetry, and the best new fashions, not just in terms of talent, but also in the "been with Jesus" factor.

The goal of Christian artists will not be to finally get the world to notice and offer big money to hijack them from their mission. They will see themselves as kingdom revolutionaries on a specific assignment from the King. They will have no compromise in them, and they will only accept exposure that allows them to keep their God assignment intact. These festivals will become massively popular, even for the world, and will serve as a major platform for evangelism as attention is drawn to the superior creativity that comes from the house of the Lord. They will bring great wealth into the house of the Lord, but that can never be the motivating factor. These festivals will be for the purpose of celebrating God and His good gifts. Accompanying guidelines will restrict the over-commercialization of the event to ensure that Christian arts festival are not done under the tutelage of Mammon. We must ensure that they are done under the banner of God as Creator.

The Prayer Strategy

Our prayer strategy involves the discovery and the removal of altars of darkness on this mountain. It involves binding the forces that are saturated with Jezebel and loosing the prophetic sources and resources of God. Jezebel, bringing seduction and death, and the Hivites, representative of perversion and counterfeiting, are the enemies. To ascend this mountain in prayer, you must have clean hands in these areas. It cannot be emphasized enough that all strategies must begin in heaven. Jesus did *only* what He saw the Father doing. Our brains can come up with logical strategies, but we must have the mind of Christ to access wisdom from above. The information we gather and the spiritual mapping we do can assist us in diagnosing arenas and centers of darkness. But the effective strategies of prayer will come to a prophetic people who understand and value hearing a live *rhema* word of the Lord.

The Action Strategy

Action must go with our prayer. God will raise up kingdom productions of movies, dramas, music, and fashion. Our greatest effectiveness against the darkness prevalent on this mountain of celebration will be turning on the light. The spirit of Elijah now coming upon God's sons and daughters will result in anointed products that will displace the darkness from the top of this mountain. The Lord will be opening doors for divine connections between fellow Elijah revolutionaries. Some will have the finances, some will have the artistic talent, some will be anointed for management, and some will have a production anointing. All will be singularly focused on God's glory expanding across the earth. The celebration mountain is all about God becoming more famous. Current, status quo Christians can't do much on this mountain because they repetitively fall to Jezebel and the Hivites as they attempt to climb. It will require Elijah revolutionaries to go after this mountain—prophetic, radical, uncompromising, holy children of the King whose primary interest is in God receiving more of the glory due to His name.

Jebusites and the Mountain of Family

ONCE AGAIN, WE'VE come to a mountain of great importance. Malachi 4:6 promises that Elijah will come and "turn the hearts of the fathers to the children, And the hearts of the children to their fathers." It's the last promise—even the last verse—of the Old Testament. Elijah will come and he will save families.

We live today among unprecedented family breakdown that has caused unprecedented social and physical ills. Many diseases can be attributed to unloving parents. (Most diseases, in fact, do have a psychosomatic source. Not all, but many do.) That means that some level of deep unhappiness weakens the immune system and makes room for a disease—a physical manifestation of an "ease" that is missing. The number one cause of emotional trauma is a dysfunctional family foundation.

The family unit is clearly under assault by Satan. More specifically, it's fathers who have failed, although Satan's assault shows up in other areas too. The mountain of family is in dire need of an infusion of Elijah revolutionaries. It could also be called the mountain of social justice because the true greatest social injustice we currently face is that the hearts of fathers are not turned toward their children and the hearts of the children are not turned towards their fathers. All other social injustices spin off of that central injustice.

Scripture says that in the last days, it's not just the parents' fault—something evil will be released on children to turn them against their parents.

> But know this, that in the last days perilous times will come: For men will be lovers of themselves, lovers of money, boasters, proud, blasphemers, *disobedient to parents, unthankful,* unholy, unloving, *unforgiving,* slanderers, *without self-control,* brutal, despisers of good, traitors, *headstrong,* haughty, lovers of pleasure rather than lovers of God.
>
> —2 TIMOTHY 3:1–4, EMPHASIS ADDED

The italicized words specifically describe the kind of children's behavior we may be familiar with, but their intensity and degree in the latter days will be worse. It is Satan's attempt to subvert the latter days work of the spirit of Elijah with a preemptive strike.

WHAT IS FAMILY?

The first definition for *family* in the dictionary is "parents and their children." That's pretty clear and simple. Family is an institution created by God. Without God's plan of morality for humans, we digress to animal and sub-animal qualities. Family and morality are the very fiber of order for society. When family order disintegrates, then social order also disintegrates; there's a direct correlation between them, as societal ills and dysfunctions have coincided with the breakdown of the family unit. Statistics on human criminality overwhelmingly indicate that broken homes are a major influence on those who become lawless. Broken homes are major contributors to drug use, illegal sexual activity, inability to secure gainful employment, jail sentences, and almost every other societal ill imaginable.

Since the father's absence or abusive behavior is the most damaging factor in a broken family unit, that's where Satan will concentrate his attack. A family unit's glue is love—first the love between husband and wife, and then the love among the family members. Without love, family cannot really exist.

Who Rules the Mountain of Family?

The seventh nation listed in Deuteronomy 7 is the Jebusite nation. The name *Jebusite* means "a place trodden down, rejection." That's the spirit on the mountain of family that must be dispossessed. The Jebusites represent rejection as it applies to our understanding of a main enemy on this mountain.

Rejection is defined as "the refusal to accept, consider, submit to, hear, receive, or admit." Its manifestation is essentially the opposite of the love described in 1 Corinthians 13. That kind of love acts as glue for marriages and for family.

> Though I speak with the tongues of men and of angels, but have not love, I have become sounding brass or a clanging cymbal. And though I have the gift of prophecy, and understand all mysteries and all knowledge, and though I have all faith, so that I could remove mountains, but have not love, I am nothing.... Love suffers long and is kind; love does not envy, love does not parade itself, is not puffed up; does not behave rudely, does not seek its own, is not provoked, thinks no evil; does not rejoice in iniquity, but rejoices in the truth; bears all things, believes all things, hopes all things, endures all things. Love never fails.... And now abide faith, hope, love, these three; but the greatest of these is love.
>
> —1 Corinthians 13:1–2, 4–8, 13

Without the help of the Lord, a person can go through a lifetime of counseling and medication and still not recover from the effects of rejection, which is just as often a lie as it is a reality. A child buys into that lie when he or she wrongly interprets the stern words or actions of a parent. In some cases, a parent's words do express rejection; for an adult, it's a brief episode of losing your cool, but for a child, rejection can really sink in. Or a parent may compare one child to another to try to motivate that child to behave better. A Jebusite demon will take advantage of these types of situations and whisper to a child that he or she is not wanted. A child can come into agreement with that lie at a very young age and live out of that rejection complex, affecting every future relationship that person is in.

A Jebusite will take advantage of every opening to sow rejection. If he sows rejection on one side of a relationship, then the person on the other side begins to reject the one they think they've been rejected by in order to protect their own heart from hurt. Very real earthquakes in a family can release seismic waves of rejection in all directions. If a husband leaves a wife, the rejection is very real and obvious and can leave incalculable damage. If there are kids, they too will absorb the rejection and take it personally. Psychologically, oldest boys tend to put the blame for a divorce on themselves and absorb it as a personal rejection. Rejection begets rejection, which begets more rejection. A person with a strong rejection complex will send out strong vibes that say, Please reject me, which then become self-fulfilling. We now have compounded relational problems in this area with multiple step-families trying to survive emotionally while all family members are carrying strong rejection baggage.

Rejection by a father (real or perceived) often comes with another severe price tag: it warps the developing sexual identity of a little boy or girl. A boy will tend to seek male approval endlessly, becoming confused and often crossing a sexual line into abnormality. In young girls, the flower of being a woman never opens, and their father's rejection commits them to a path of never needing anything from a man again. When the Jebusite demons can do this level of emotional damage, then they have prepared their prey for the principality atop this mountain.

WHO IS KING OF THE JEBUSITES?

The principality who sits atop the mountain of family is Baal. He and Jezebel are very similar, but Baal is more encompassing. Jezebel serves Baal. The nations surrounding Israel had their own versions of Baal that were a constant snare to God's people.

The name Baal means "master," "owner," or "lord." He was the god of fertility, the sun god, the god of provision, the god of rain, and looked

168

to for basically everything. The cult of Baal worship often included male prostitution. Service to the god Molech was also connected with Baal worship, as we can see in Jeremiah:

> They built the high places of Baal which are in the Valley of the Son of Hinnom, to cause their sons to pass through the fire to Molech.
>
> —JEREMIAH 32:35

One could serve Baal by serving Molech, the one to whom children were brutally and cruelly sacrificed. In one example, worshipers would heat up statues of Molech and then place their children in the statues' red-hot arms and watch the children burn to death. For us, this represents the prevailing god and influence of abortion. Since the Roe v. Wade ruling in 1973, almost fifty million children have been sacrificed at this altar of convenience.[1] Baal worship in our land has cost millions their life. Abortion is the rejection of a child by a parent, evidence of the Jebusites of rejection at work. We see the heart of a parent turned not toward their children, but rather against them in a deadly way.

Homosexuality is also a manifestation of Baal worship and explains why male prostitution was integral to Baal ceremonies. Homosexuality is the rejection of one's natural sex drive. This rejection isn't necessarily a conscious choice; it's the fruit of rejection that has been sown in someone and defiled him. The point is not whether one is born homosexual or not. God's standards of morality reflect the feelings we must be trained into, not the feelings we were born with. None of us were born with His standards bubbling up in us.

For example, we are all naturally selfish. That's something that must be trained out of us. For most of us, it's a lifetime fight, as the me-first feeling seems wired into us. Because of this selfishness, we easily feel angry, sad, jealous, vengeful, and just plain mean. These inherent feelings we're born with must be corrected by embracing God's higher authority of righteous morality. All of the descriptions of love in 1 Corinthians 13 are anti-natural feelings. To bear with, believe, forgive, endure, think no wrong—none come naturally.

So why do we deify a natural sexual drive as God-ordained? It isn't. None of us, heterosexual or homosexual, is born with a monogamous sex drive, but that doesn't justify fornication and adultery. Some apparently think they are born with feelings toward pedophilia or even bestiality. If a sex drive is self-validating, as many assume, then we really begin to stray into apostasy.

Having said all that, I do recognize that demons are on assignment to warp our sexual psyches when we are young so that we'll have inordinate and confused sex drives. Studies show that most porn stars and strip club dancers were sexually abused by a close male figure when they were young. That's also true for a high percentage of homosexuals. This is tragic, but is certainly no reason to validate sexual deviance.

God will begin to release a new level of power for healing and restoration through and into His people at depths few have been able to experience. I am very aware that many, if not most, with homosexual feelings have cried and pleaded with God to no longer have these feelings. The powerlessness of the church has been complicit in this overall problem, and the spirit of Elijah will bring that power back. Homosexuals will come back to the church en masse and submit to special prayers for restoration when the word gets out that *total* sexual healing is really available in God's house. Many feel hopeless about their sex drive because nothing they have experienced so far has dimmed the deviancy. The combination of embracing His standards, whether we feel them or not, and the new power of God coming to His church will provide true, undeniable deliverance for hundreds of thousands of homosexuals. This will be among the primary evidence that the Elijah Revolution is upon us in full measure.

It's interesting that the homosexual activist agenda is about acceptance. They band together and find cities of acceptance. Their legal and political maneuverings aim to let them finally function under some level of social acceptance. The internal rejection is so profound that they must attempt extreme natural measures to make that rejection bearable. Though the gay agenda is wrong and very damaging, it's very understandable. It's also a reminder to us, as the church, that we have done very little to bring heaven's answers to a significant hurting segment of society. We are going to have to learn how to bring God's love and power to gay communities, while still warning them of the profound judgments of God that will come their way if they should continue to embrace their sins. To stay locked in homosexuality is to remain in worship of Baal—and it is specifically Baal who is about to suffer profound repercussions brought on by the Elijah Revolution.

THE WORSHIP OF BAAL AND JUDGMENTS

As mentioned in a previous chapter, I wrote a prophetic newsletter in October 2004 (before Katrina) warning of judgments coming to a stretch of land from Mobile to New Orleans. I wrote that an altar to Baal existed between these cities and that Mobile, Biloxi, and New Orleans all carried stones of this altar. Mardi Gras began in Mobile back in 1699, though New Orleans has become more famous for it. The origins of Mardi Gras come from the fertility festival of Lupercalia, which has direct roots to Baal worship. Mardi Gras is essentially a celebration of Baal. I wrote that the next hurricanes would be the judgment storms, and that New Orleans was headed for a "big uneasy." I also wrote, "Biloxi: The Eye of a Hurricane Has Your Name on It." I shared that the hurricanes of 2004 were warning storms of what would be God's manifest judgments on Baal's altar at that geographical area of our nation.

A mass homosexual parade and celebration that was to bring many millions of dollars to New Orleans was scheduled the week Katrina hit the city. Baal was doubling up in the city by adding homosexual decadence to his existing active altar there. Hurricanes Wilma and Rita also each brought judgment on cities that were about to host major gay events—Key West and Cancun—thus seriously curtailing the celebration of gay acceptance. God loves homosexuals so much that he will spare no expense in making it clear that homosexuality is an abomination to Him and that He can deliver someone from it. The name Katrina even means "purity"—perhaps a message of God's intent for that hurricane. What looks like God's anger against homosexuals is really His passionate love working to spare them from greater judgment—lifetime in a real hell:

When Your judgments are in the earth, The inhabitants of the world will learn righteousness. Let grace be shown to the wicked, Yet he will not learn righteousness. In the land of uprightness he will deal unjustly, And will not behold the majesty of the LORD.

—ISAIAH 26:9–10

There is a point when grace ceases to reap a reward, and we are at that point in many areas of societal sin. We have entered a time when His righteous judgments must be made evident so that the wicked can learn righteousness. We are headed into a season when the Lord will entreat the gay community with His judgments so they will learn righteousness. Nobody understands more than the Lord the tragic rejections that homosexuals have had to endure. Nobody is cheering more for them to overcome these challenges of life. Yet sin cannot go unpunished, and abominations receive the more severe judgments of God. To be tempted with feelings of homosexuality is not an abomination to Him, but crossing the line into actual homosexual behavior is.

So Baal is the principality of the mountain of family and his demons of entrance are the Jebusites of rejection. Abortion and homosexuality are forms of worship that strengthen Baal, and his goal is the disintegration of the family, which he knows will in turn disintegrate society. In the last days, the mountain of the Lord's house will dethrone him, and we are now in those days.

THE IMPORTANT ROLE OF PASTORS

Taking this mountain will fast-forward as God's true pastors begin taking their proper places. The people we now call pastors are far removed from what this ministry is designed to do. We traditionally view a pastor as someone who heads up a church and preaches the message of the week. It is more biblically correct for apostles and prophets to lead the church and for pastors be the very hands-on ministers of God's mercy and grace. (See Ephesians 2:20.) Their strength is not administration, not necessarily even teaching, and not laying out vision, but rather in having a heart that has been conditioned to apply the one-on-one personal care of the Lord. Many such pastors also attempt to do all the things that running and leading a church requires—which is why burnout is such a problem among pastors, with a reported fifteen thousand quitting every year.

As churches become more biblically ordered, many more pastors than we presently have will be discovered and commissioned. They will be unencumbered by financial considerations and therefore free to love on God's lambs with no concern for remuneration. There is nothing more polluted than a pastor who is a hireling. (See John 10:12–13.)

WOMEN PASTORS

Another reason we are so pastorally weak is that we have excluded or limited women from stepping into this role. Women often seem more wired for intercession than men, and this is also the case with pastoring—perhaps even more so. Many women have a natural gift for nurturing, and when we finally recognize enough of them in their proper role, we will have a church that much better represents the heart of our Good Shepherd.

MARKETPLACE PASTORS

Beside the change that is coming into the church ranks itself are changes that will come to the extended church—the church in the marketplace, where these seven mountains will be actively taken. The mountain of family must be infiltrated by pastors in every sector of society. Regardless of your title at your place of employment, you may be called to serve as pastor of that workplace. Your specific assignment is to displace the Jebusites by bringing the healing, redemption, and acceptance of Christ to wherever you may be. Rejection is the door that opens people to all sorts of Baal complications. We must deal with it in its early stages, and then we must be empowered to bring God's might to set Baal's captives free.

GOVERNMENT SERVICES PASTORS

Government services that assist families are one of our primary areas of need. The Department of Family and Children Services should be staffed entirely by pastors—not official, professional pastors, but those who see this mountain of society as their mission field. Many Christians have no desire to enter that arena because the pay is weak and the positions carry no prestige. That's why the task requires true shepherds, not hirelings, in the social infrastructure of our nation. This is a clarion call to Elijah revolutionaries to enter this arena and begin to bring the reign and rule of God to Earth.

JUDGES WHO ARE PASTORS

Judges are granted great latitude to intervene in personal family issues. The kingdom would be best served if judgeships were filled by sons and daughters of God who understand the King's ways. Only Holy Spirit-filled judges can have the proper instinct for how much mercy or justice to dispense. We need judges who know that God really considers them pastors and are willing to bring His light in this way.

LEVELS OF THE MOUNTAIN

We have already addressed the fact that Baal and the Jebusites are the spiritual influences on the top of this mountain. The physical faces are not as clear as those on other mountains. Laws that govern family relationships, however, are clearly up there. Laws are important in the sense that they represent the government's tacit approval of behavior. Government then becomes accountable before God for the laws on the books. For example, some abortions will occur even if there's a law against it. But if a government sets no standard of righteousness on the matter, then it is called into account for the sins of the people—and not just the individual sinners. Therefore, laws and ordinances that govern the family—and, by extension, those who have power to change laws and ordinances—sit at the top of this mountain.

The Supreme Court is probably even more influential on the mountain of family than on the mountain of politics. It decided *Roe v. Wade* and is the only entity with the power to reverse it. Its justices have the power to determine, for legal purposes, what a family is. They are involved in all morality-related rulings. To fully dethrone Baal and take this mountain, we will have to bring His influence to the Supreme Court. The emerging Elijah Revolution will begin to bring God's order to the top of this mountain.

Less influential judgeships that have significant authority in family legal issues are probably at the mid-mountain level. On the low level of the mountain is the presence of God's people as pastors in every segment and fabric of society—particularly those involved in government family services.

WHAT DOES THE BIBLE SAY ABOUT FAMILY?

The Bible uses the word *family* 123 times and the word *families* 174 times. The Lord clearly establishes Himself as the God of families. Even the Trinity reflects a family dynamic. There is Father and Son, and the role of the Holy Spirit is to prepare a bride for the Son for the marriage supper of the Lamb. (See Revelation 19:9.) His heart towards relational life is further expressed in Psalm 68:

> A father of the fatherless, a defender of widows, Is God in His holy habitation. God sets the solitary in families; He brings out those who are bound into prosperity.
>
> —PSALM 68: 5–6

God's heart is the heart of a family man. The members of the Trinity communed among themselves as the world was created. They then made Adam, who, since he was in the image of this Trinity, was lonely without a family identity. In Psalm 68, God announces Himself as "father of the fatherless." He knew that man would fail in His model, so He provided Himself as the Father of the fatherless. To a widow who has lost her husband, He is her defender and even her husband, as He says in Isaiah 54:5. The passage above states that "God sets the solitary in families." We are all solitary by nature, but He has put us in families to bring forth fruitfulness as we live a proper family life. The greatest individual on the earth can reproduce nothing outside of the context of family. The Elijah Revolution will recover and reveal the beauty of family. The hearts of parents and their children will be turned toward each other.

> Behold, I will send you Elijah the prophet Before the great and dreadful day of the LORD. And he will turn The hearts of the fathers to the children, And the hearts of the children to their fathers, Lest I come and strike the earth with a curse.
>
> —MALACHI 4:5–6

We haven't touched on that last phrase yet, but it's important. If this family restoration doesn't come, the earth will be struck with a curse. That word *curse* means "annihilation." The earth will suffer annihilation if true family is not restored on Earth. AIDS is a disease that has its roots in the violation of God's mores for the family. It's a sin disease that decimates families and leaves millions of orphans behind. A man and a woman who marry as virgins have provided themselves with the ultimate protection against AIDS. There are, of course, many innocent AIDS carriers, but the source of the disease is sinful, anti-family behavior. Forty million people in the world are now infected with a death sentence that is directly attributable to violating God's known standards for family life. Could the curse of Malachi 4:6 be an even worse disease or virus that takes out the disobedient? Elijah revolutionaries will not stand by and allow that possibility to unfold. We will receive and carry the restorative work of the spirit of Elijah to the nations.

A MULTI-PRONGED APPROACH

We've already addressed many aspects of the multi-pronged approach. The important thing is to realize that it *is* a multi pronged approach. We can't just pursue prayer or action; we have to cover both. Within these two broad approaches are several strategies. The infiltration of the multiple levels that we've mentioned is key. We need to find our row of favor and anointing and begin marching in that row. The top of the mountain must be flooded with Elijah revolutionaries, and those who do will find the most favor backing them up. It is time for the Lord's house to be exalted—and for all other infrastructures to collapse—leading the nations to *run* to the house of the Lord.

THE PRAYER STRATEGY

Intense prayer for the Supreme Court is obviously a high priority. It's important for us to understand and believe in faith that we can legislate in the spirit realm, even with the wrong people in office. If we don't understand this fact, we will only gear up in prayer for moments of election and selection and think we have won or lost based on that event.

The book of Esther reminds us of the power of intercession. Ahasuerus was historically considered an evil man, yet through Esther's intercession he made righteous decrees that greatly benefited God's people. Conversely, we've had Supreme Court justices who have seemed to be the right people, but who, once under the powers of influence at the top of the mountain, started voting against what is right and just. We must break through in prayer and create an umbrella of influence in the Spirit where righteous enactments are made regardless of who is in office. Baal must be knocked out of Washington, D.C., and a prevailing influence of God-consciousness must be raised so that the fear of the Lord begins to instruct Supreme Court justices. We have to work to have evil or deceived justices removed, of course; but the key is to remove Baal through prayer. Intercession is a powerful weapon for taking the Supreme Court and this mountaintop.

THE ACTION STRATEGY

Several action strategies have already been laid out. We need both preventative strategies and redemptive strategies. By preventative strategies, I mean establishing or defending laws that strengthen the family unit. By redemptive strategies, I mean finding ways to restore, rebuild, and recover family life that has been lost.

Statistical evidence overwhelmingly indicates that our welfare laws are actually harmful to the family unit. Some adjustments have been made, but more are needed. Any law that financially remunerates those who have children out of wedlock—and then benefits them more if they do *not* marry—has negative effects on the family unit. The welfare laws that make it financially advantageous to have no job (as opposed to a low paying job), inadvertently promote lifelong dependence on welfare, which is not healthy either for an individual or a family. Whoever has the opportunity and the favor to tackle these legal issues should approach the overhaul of this system from the standpoint of what would most promote and strengthen a strong family unit. The financial factors cannot be the primary consideration for determining good law. God's grace will accompany efforts to implement righteous change.

The devastating problem of orphans in the world has already reached a critical stage and will only increase. There are millions of AIDS orphans in Africa alone—children whose nuclear family unit has been irrevocably destroyed. There are also orphans from war and combat situations. There are an estimated two hundred fifty thousand child soldiers in the world, and most of them are orphans. This problem of children without a home and family breaks the Lord's heart.

Some Elijah revolutionaries will be blessed with strategies and income to create an entirely new orphanage model. Orphanages that carry the spirit of Elijah's anointing on them will be able to provide supernatural healing and restoration for their orphans— something that carries the DNA of the family of heaven. Some really good models are already out there, but a spiritual upgrade is even available. Kingdom orphanages will produce not only survivors of horrible trauma, but will also be the very place from which champions on the tops of the mountains will come from. Those whom Satan has stolen the most from will be granted authority and favor to cause him the most damage. Some of society's most incredible mighty men (and women) of the future are currently devastated orphans. Great grace is available for those who will extend themselves to reach these beloved children of God. His heart is always stirred most strongly toward the fatherless, the rejected, and those with no hope of a future except in Him. It's time to tackle this mountain and bring God's unshakeable kingdom to it.

The Head and
Not the Tail

The LORD will make you the head and not the tail; you shall be above only, and not be beneath, if you heed the commandments of the LORD your God.

—DEUTERONOMY 28:13

I

T IS IMPORTANT that we, God's blood-bought people, realize that it has always been His will for us to be at the top of the mountains in a place of preeminence and blessing. He is not a sadistic God who loves seeing His people struggle and barely survive. Nothing could be further from the truth. He has always sought to motivate us with a promised land of unlimited abundance—body, soul, and spirit. He wants to give us that for two reasons. First, He is a great and loving Father who loves to shower His kids with blessings. Second, His blessings are His ultimate demonstration before principalities and powers of the conclusive truth that love never fails. All He has ever demanded in return is that we obey His commandments.

We have long known and acknowledged the Ten Commandments (though even His own people have not always done very well with them). These commandments, however, did not express the primary passion of God's heart for His people. His purpose and desire for Israel was the commandment to enter the Promised Land. They did not embrace this purpose for an entire generation. Instead, they lived as "the tail" because of their disobedience to the command to enter Canaan and dispossess the "seven nations greater and mightier than thou."

Israel disobeyed this commandment because life in Egypt had conditioned them to be faithless. They remembered being held in captivity by one nation that controlled their every move. Now God was challenging them to believe that they could dominate *seven* nations, all greater and mightier than they were. They had no faith to believe His promises because they were locked in unbelief.

Hebrews 3 gives us a New Testament perspective:

> "Today, if you will hear His voice, Do not harden your hearts as in the rebellion, In the day of trial in the wilderness, Where your fathers tested Me, tried Me, And saw My works forty years. Therefore I was angry with that generation, And said, 'They always go astray in their heart, And they have not known My ways, So I swore in My wrath, They shall not enter My rest.'" Beware, brethren, lest there be in any of you an evil heart of unbelief…For who, having heard, rebelled. Indeed, was it not all who came out of Egypt, led by Moses? Now with whom was He angry forty years? Was it not with those who sinned, whose corpses fell in the wilderness? And to whom did He swear that they would not enter His rest, but to those who did not obey? So we see that they could not enter in because of unbelief.
>
> —HEBREWS 3:7–12, 16–19

The Lord viewed the entire forty-year period as "in the rebellion." He provided manna from heaven, He gave water from the rock, He protected them from their enemies—but it was all "in the rebellion." We will one day look back at the two thousand years since Christ and realize that it was all in the rebellion. Our rebellion hasn't been against the Ten Commandments. It is in having hearts of unbelief that God could use us to dispossess seven nations greater and mightier than us. This was Israel's evil heart, the sin from which every other sin manifested. When we default from our purpose and assignment, we are subject to sins that are begotten from being in the rebellion. Israel fell to Baal, golden calves, and murmuring and complaining because they were not on their mission. They did not embrace God's commandment to possess the land, so they remained the tail and not the head. They stayed below and not above.

WHAT DOES IT LOOK LIKE TO BE THE HEAD?

Deuteronomy 28 tells us what it looks like to be the head:

> Blessed shall you be in the city, and blessed shall you be in the country. Blessed shall be the fruit of your body, the produce of your ground and the increase of your herds, the increase of your cattle and the offspring of your flocks. Blessed shall be your basket and your kneading bowl. Blessed shall you be when you come in, and blessed shall you be when you go out. The LORD will cause your enemies who rise against you to be defeated before your face; they shall come against you one way and flee before you seven ways. The LORD will command the blessing on you in your store-houses, and in all which you set your hand, and He will bless you in the land which the LORD your God is giving you.
>
> —DEUTERONOMY 28:3–8

The Lord describes blessing in every conceivable way. It even extends to the defeat of all enemies who rise against them. This is clearly and pointedly what life in the promised land is supposed to look like. The enemy will "flee before you seven ways." Though the seven nations are greater and mightier than you, they will run away in seven directions. This promise of blessing is not something to be "named and claimed" while we are committed only to life in the wilderness. That's the central error of the prosperity message—that God wants us to have and be all these things in the wilderness. Only in the active conquest of the seven greater nations will He bless us like this. And there's more:

> The LORD will establish you as a holy people to Himself, just as He has sworn to you, if you keep the commandments of the LORD your God and walk in His ways. Then all the peoples of the

earth shall see that you are called by the name of the LORD, and they shall be afraid of you. And the LORD will grant you plenty of goods, in the fruit of your body, in the increase of your live-stock, and in the produce of your ground, in the land of which the Lord swore to your fathers to give to you.

—DEUTERONOMY 28:9–11

The great work to be accomplished for people holy to the Lord will be intimacy with Him. God's great desire is for the peoples of the earth to see how good a God He is to those who serve Him. We will be rich in God Himself in every conceivable way that prosperity and blessing can be described—but it's "in the land which the Lord swore to your fathers to give you." This has always been in God's heart for every generation. Yet all along, He has known that this group of Elijah revolutionaries would not cross over Jordan for about two thousand "cubits," or years (see Joshua 3:4), after the ark (Jesus).

The promises of Deuteronomy 28 are not for those who are looking to the rapture as their exit strategy from planet Earth. These promises are not for those who have no faith to see the kingdoms of this world become the kingdoms of our God. These blessings are not for those who live as citizens of Earth with only a secondary allegiance to the King. These blessings are not for those who are risking nothing and exercising no faith. They are not for those who are fighting enemies they *can* defeat. These blessings are for those who have enlisted to take the seven greater and mightier nations—those willing to take on the seven mountains of media, economy, religion, government, education, celebration, and family. This is for those who can look at Apollyon and his Hittites of Fear; at Lucifer and his Girgashites of Corruption; at Beel-zebub and his Amorites of Humanism; at Mammon and his Canaanites of Greed; at the Religious Spirit and his Perizzites of Idolatry; at Jezebel and her Hivites of Perversion; and at Baal and his Jebusites of Rejec-tion—and can say, as Joshua and Caleb did, "They are our bread."

Joshua the son of Nun and Caleb the son of Jephunneh...spoke to all the congregation of the children of Israel, saying: "The land we passed through to spy out is an exceedingly good land. If the

LORD delights in us, then He will bring us into this land and give it to us, 'a land which flows milk and honey.' Only do not rebel against the LORD, nor fear the people of the land, for they are our bread; their protection has departed from them, and the LORD is with us. Do not fear them."

—NUMBERS 14:6–9

Only two men out of all those who had been in Egypt could see with the Lord's perspective. Only two saw the exceedingly good land. Only two knew that to fear the seven great nations was to be in rebellion. Only Joshua and Caleb saw the impossible enemies as forces whose protection had already departed from them—even forty years before they were engaged in combat. The rest of Israel saw unapproachable giants, but these men saw the giants as food for getting stronger. Getting rid of the *-ites* was, to them, like eating bread. Did this resonate at all with the children of Israel?

And all the congregation said to stone them with stones.

—NUMBERS 14:10

Joshua and Caleb were not only verbally disdained for their suggestion that maybe God could actually give the nations to those who ask Him, Israel attempted to shut them up forever. They wanted them dead for suggesting that God could give them more than the emergency rations He had given in the wilderness.

Their disdain and fear echoes through the generations: "How dare they challenge the doctrinal status quo of life in the desert. How dare they believe in a God who can take a nation in a day. How dare they believe in a God who can perform even 'greater works' through His sons than He Himself performed. How dare they believe in such a large and powerful God. These voices must be silenced, because some of the younger generation might begin to believe these unrealistic expectations—and then we're all in trouble. They have no sense of history or tradition, and may end up believing that all things are possible. Next thing you know, they will start prophesying to mountains and telling them to be removed. (See Mark 11:23.) What's next, prophesying to dry bones and expecting life? No, this is dangerous. If we believe Joshua and Caleb, we're going to have to toss out all of our books and manuals on eschatology. No, this kind of talk could start a revolution."

RECEIVING THE DIFFERENT SPIRIT

When we look at the life of Joshua and Caleb to see how they could view things so differently than an entire nation, we only get one significant biblical clue.

> My servant Caleb, because he has a different spirit in him, and has followed Me fully, I will bring into the land where he went, and his descendants shall inherit it.
> —NUMBERS 14:24

This spirit is the very same spirit the Lord is now releasing. It's the spirit of Elijah that will come and turn average nobodies into Elijah revolutionaries who fear nothing except falling short in their faith in a big God. When this different spirit rests upon you, your God grows to be huge, and giants all of a sudden turn into bread to be eaten. If this good God-virus has taken you, you will begin to burn with new hopes and expectations of His greatness on Earth. You will begin to run across the Jordan, embracing the death of your old identity of just being saved and waiting for His return to now being saved *and* hastening His return. (See 2 Peter 3:12.)

We hasten Jesus' return by fulfilling the assignment He has given us. He will continue to let generation after generation die—and not return—until one generation gets the assignment and performs His will on Earth as it is in heaven. Acts 3:21 tells us that Jesus is held in the heaven "until the times of restoration of all things," specifically that which He spoke "by the mouth of all His holy prophets since the world began." What have the prophets been speaking ever since the world began? Subdue the earth, have dominion over every living thing that moves on the earth. (See Genesis 1:28.) Demonic powers are also living things that move on the earth, and until a generation rises to fulfill the original mission of subduing and dominating them, Jesus is held in the heavens. He will not return until all is accomplished. You can pray for His return until you are blue in the face, but He's not coming back until someone finishes the assignment. He is sitting in intercession for us at the right hand of the Father until all His enemies are put under our feet. (See Psalm 47:3 and Romans 16:20.) Once His enemies are crushed, every good thing that God has intended to take place here on Earth will be restored. Only then can we get in that "He could come back any day" delusion some are already in.

THE SEVEN SPIRITS OF GOD FOR THE SEVEN MOUNTAINS

Revelation 1:4 refers to the seven spirits of God. We see the term again in Revelation 3:1. It shows up again in the next chapter. From the throne proceeded lightnings, thunderings, and voices. Seven lamps of fire were burning before the throne, which are the seven spirits of God. (See Revelation 4:5.)

Finally, it appears one last time in the following chapter:

> I looked, and behold, in the midst of the throne and of the four living creatures, and in the midst of the elders, stood a Lamb as though it had been slain, having seven horns and seven eyes, which are the seven spirits of God sent out into all the earth.
>
> —REVELATION 5:6

It is through the Lamb who was slain and because of Him that seven spirits of God have been sent into the whole earth. These seven spirits have a mission *on Earth*. They don't remain in heaven. The seven spirits have seven horns and seven eyes—horns representing power and authority, eyes representing the prophetic gift. The seven spirits are the spirit of Elijah prophesied in Malachi. It's the same prophetic power and anointing that rested on Elijah. Revelation 19:10 tells us that "the testimony of Jesus is the spirit of prophecy." Power (horns) and seeing (eyes) come together in Him. As we receive the mind of Christ for the end times, our eyes are enlightened to understand just how much authority and power He has granted the saints here on Earth.

The eyes of your understanding being enlightened; that you may know what is the hope of His calling, what are the riches of the glory of His inheritance in the saints, and what is the exceeding greatness of His power toward us who believe, according to the working of His mighty power which He worked in Christ when He raised Him from the dead and seated Him at His right hand in the heavenly places, far above all principality and power and might and dominion, and every name that is named, not only in this age but also in that which is to come.

—EPHESIANS 1:18–23

As the eyes of understanding are enlightened, we begin to inherit the greatness of His power. We receive the spirit of Elijah by receiving the seven spirits of God that testify of a glorious inheritance available in the saints. Then we see the end result of the seven spirits of God being released on the earth:

And have made us kings and priests to our God; And we shall reign on earth.

—REVELATION 5:10

This isn't over until we reign on Earth. Genesis starts with, "Have dominion over everything," and Revelation ends with, "We shall reign on earth." The Lamb that was slain provides the seven spirits of God that bring the seven horns of power over the seven nations greater and mightier than us. That's why it's incidental that they are greater and mightier than us. He has released the seven horns of power to topple every rebellious spirit that has exalted itself against the Creator. The seven eyes release the prophetic vision to understand that this is our inheritance on Earth. The earth will continue to shift and quake with expectation and birth pangs. It will cause a series of tsunamis that will totally transform the face of the earth. All destructible structures will come down. Everything that can be shaken will be shaken. But the sons and daughters of the kingdom will be on the mountaintops and will receive the unshakeable kingdom. Then will be the end of all rebellion on Earth.

Notes

Chapter 7

AMORITES AND THE MOUNTAIN OF EDUCATION

1. Howard Kurtz, "College Faculties a Mostly Liberal Lot, Study Finds," *Washington Post*, March 29, 2005.

2. See http://www.viewzone.com/bicam.html (accessed November 30, 2007).

Chapter 8

CANAANITES AND THE MOUNTAIN OF ECONOMY

1. See http://stocks.ezguide2.com/ (accessed November 30, 2007).

2. See http://www.nrlc.org/abortion/facts/abortionstats.html (accessed November 30, 2007).

Chapter 9

PERIZZITES AND THE MOUNTAIN OF RELIGION

1. See http://www.adherents.com/Religions_By_Adherents.html (accessed November 30, 2007).

Chapter 10

HIVITES AND THE MOUNTAIN OF CELEBRATION

1. See http://www.burntout.com/kurt/biography/ (accessed November 30, 2007).

Chapter 11

JEBUSITES AND THE MOUNTAIN OF FAMILY

1. See http://www.nrlc.org/abortion/facts/abortionstats.html (accessed November 30, 2007).

The Seven Mountain Prophecy Quick Reference Chart

Mountain	Enemy on the Mountain	Principality on the Mountain	Significant Displacing Authority	Basic Mission	Revelation 5:12 Key
Media	Hittites *(represent bad news)*	Apollyon (destroyer)	Evangelists	Fill the airwaves with "good news"	Blessing
Government	Girgashites *(represent corruption)*	Lucifer (pride and manipulation)	Apostles	Fill government positions with humble, servant, integrous leaders	Power
Education	Amorites *(represent humanism)*	Beelzebub (lies)	Teachers	Bring in new fear-of-God-based curriculum	Wisdom

Economy	Canaanites *(represent love of money)*	Mammon *(greed)*	Prophets	Discover and transfer wealth into kingdom purposes	Riches
Celebration	Hivites *(represent compro- mise)*	Jezebel *(seduction)*	Prophets	Model the greater creative arts of God and prophesy through them	Glory
Religion	Perizzites *(represent idolatry)*	The religious spirit *(false worship)*	Holy Spirit	Model a Holy- Spirit- infused life and ministry	Honor
Family	Jebusites *(represent rejection)*	Baal *(perversion)*	Pastors	Impact social systems so that the family unit is prioritized	Strength

The Seven Mountain Prophecy Quick
Reference Overview

CHAPTER 1: TSUNAMI!

Just as the Asian tsunami of 2004 suddenly raised the sea level and changed the landscape of everything in its path, so is a coming spiritual tsunami going to suddenly transform the world as we know it. But the outcome of this tsunami will be anything but disastrous. It will bring God's rule and reign to bear in places that have been dominated and devastated by evil powers of darkness.

CHAPTER 2: AN ELIJAH REVOLUTION

The world and the church are in need of an extreme makeover. The coming Elijah Revolution will have transforming dynamics as powerful as a tsunami, and it will affect the entire world—including the church. This move of God will have all the characteristics of the ministry of Elijah. It will be prophetic and powerful, and it will prepare the way of the Lord before His return. According to Scripture, Jesus will sit at God's right hand until all of His enemies are put under His feet. The Elijah Revolution will accomplish this.

CHAPTER 3: THRUST INTO THE PROMISED LAND

The Elijah Revolution will take us into our promised land. As we follow the ark of God's presence—in the book of Joshua, God's people followed two thousand cubits behind the ark; our generation follows Christ's ministry on Earth by two thousand years—we will be led in unfamiliar ways. Our promised land is the nations, all of which rightfully belong to God. As we pursue His mission, we will experience promised-land provision. Manna from heaven and water from the rock were only wilderness provisions. We will receive the abundance of God's promise in order to fulfill His calling.

CHAPTER 4: SEVEN NATIONS GREATER AND MIGHTIER

As the Lord brings us into our promised land, we will encounter seven nations "greater and mightier" than us. (Deuteronomy 7:1.) Joshua's enemies were the Hittites, the Girgashites, the Amorites, the Canaanites, the Perizzites, the Hivites, and the Jebusites. For us, those nations correspond to seven "mountains" that shape society: media, government, education, economy, religion, celebration and arts, and family. These mountains were once revealed separately but simultaneously to Loren Cunningham and Bill Bright as keys to transforming nations. With God-given strategies and power, Elijah revolutionaries will have unprecedented favor to displace the evil principalities on these mountains and occupy them with kingdom citizens.

CHAPTER 5: HITTITES AND THE MOUNTAIN OF MEDIA

The word Hittite comes from a word meaning "terror" and "fear"— exactly the characteristics of modern news media, which focuses overwhelmingly on negative news and even decides which negative stories get the most airtime and headlines. The principality Apollyon (meaning "destroyer"), who sits atop the mountain of media, twists news and enslaves people by magnifying their fears. Elijah revolutionaries, who will function essentially as true evangelists, will report news accurately, even when it's bad news, but will be able to find the redemptive angle in every story. Their words will powerfully prophesy the blessings of God to the world.

CHAPTER 6: GIRGASHITES AND THE MOUNTAIN OF GOVERNMENT

Most people consider politics to be "of the devil." That's because Christians have abandoned it to the devil. The Girgashites, whose name means "dwelling in clay soil," represent the earthly desires and corrupt ambitions common to this mountain. Lucifer, the prince of this mountain, will be displaced by those who ascend it in a spirit opposite to his pride, a spirit of humility and service. True apostles—not those who have a business card that carries the title "apostle," but those who function in that role as Scripture defines it—will be instrumental in the taking of the mountain of government. They will understand that "of the increase of [Jesus'] government there will be no end" (Isa. 9:7).

CHAPTER 7: AMORITES AND THE MOUNTAIN OF EDUCATION

Highly influential educational institutions that began centuries ago as Christian colleges and universities are now saturated in liberal, humanistic philosophies. The mountain of education is dominated by schools like Harvard, Yale, and Princeton, each of which has educated numerous world leaders. The Amorites on this mountain, who represent pride, boasting, and haughtiness, characterize the man-exalting ideals of humanism, liberalism, rationalism, and atheism. God's judgments will soon be clear enough that people will stop wondering if there is a God and ask instead what they should do about His existence.

A prevailing flaw in all educational systems is the emphasis on left-brain understanding of truth. Extreme prejudice against right-brain ways of thinking transform the vast majority of children from those who are able to receive creative, imaginative, intuitive revelation from God to those who are rationalistic, critical, and so limited to the five human senses that they can't receive God's revelation. The Elijah Revolution will dethrone Beelzebub from this mountain, turn education back to a right-brain dominant enterprise, and open the way for children to discern the presence of God and prophesy His mysteries.

CHAPTER 8: CANAANITES AND THE MOUNTAIN OF ECONOMY

The twin lies of greed and poverty both grow out of the influence of the principalities of Mammon, or Babylon. This lying spirit convinces people everywhere that money is their true source of provision. It prefers to enslave people in poverty, but where God blesses with abundance, it twists abundance into greed for more. But the economic systems of this world will one day collapse, and all who have operated under this spirit of poverty and greed will be left with nothing to depend on except God.

God calls His people to come out of this system. Those who depend exclusively on Him will "eat the wealth of nations." Abundance will come as a result of faith in the prophetic words God gives through His servants—a dynamic demonstrated often in Scripture (through men like Joseph, Elijah, Elisha) and in my own experiences in Honduras, Costa Rica, Peru, and elsewhere. Babylon will be shaken until it collapses, but those who trust in the Lord will suffer no lack.

CHAPTER 9: PERIZZITES AND THE MOUNTAIN OF RELIGION

Idolatry strips people of their provision and protection—words that reflect the meaning of the Perizzites' name—by placing them in submission to gods that can't and won't deliver on their empty promises. The spirit of religion atop the mountain of religion does everything it can to steal worship that rightfully belongs to God, whether through blatant worship of Satan, subtle religiosity within the church, or anything in between. This spirit distorts our worship with lying doctrines that seem true but are mixed with poison. Even mature Christians can stall out in their worship by focusing on a mountaintop experience or exalting a doctrine over a real relationship with God.

This chapter teaches readers that this mountain can only be taken through the dynamic leading and power of the Holy Spirit. Elijah revolutionaries will expect the Spirit to work in unexpected ways and be sensitive to His voice. Wildly, passionately in love with the Lord, they will refuse to practice a religion based on platitudes and principles, well-scheduled worship services, and neat and tidy theology. They will instead have supernatural experiences with God that defy the expectations and traditions of status quo Christianity.

CHAPTER 10: HIVITES AND THE MOUNTAIN OF CELEBRATION

The mountain of celebration includes the arts, music, sports, fashion, entertainment, and every other way we celebrate and enjoy life. This mountain has so thoroughly been captured by Satan's hordes that most believers aren't sure it can even be possessed. But God's Spirit wants to move freely through the creativity and passion of His people. This mountain must be taken from the Hivites, who counterfeit true celebration with corrupt substitutes, and from the spirit of Jezebel that seduces many away from the true pleasure and joy offered by God. The spirit of Jezebel prostitutes the good gifts of God, and the role of prophets will be to see through the deceptions of pop culture and offer the real and lasting alternative to our society, especially its youth, who live and breathe on this mountain during their teen years. Elijah revolutionaries will produce music, art, literature, and every other form of celebration the Lord's way—by being in His presence and letting His creativity flow through them. The world will begin to value and pursue the gift that Christian artists have because the quality of their work will point to a supernatural source.

CHAPTER 11: JEBUSITES AND THE MOUNTAIN OF FAMILY

Malachi 4:6 promises that Elijah will come and "turn the hearts of the fathers to the children, And the hearts of the children to their fathers" (NKJV). It's the last promise—even the last verse—of the Old Testament. Elijah will come, and he will save families. It's clear that families are under assault; we live in an era of unprecedented family breakdown. At the center of this problem is lack of fathers who are fully engaged in the life of their family. The result is numerous social and physical ills that spring out of rejection, including depression, fear, sexual deviance, addictions, anger, and violence.

The principality on this mountain is Baal, the worship of whom often involved sexual rituals and child sacrifice. The true role of pastors—in the marketplace, government (especially the judiciary branch), as well as in churches—will be instrumental in removing Baal from the mountain of family and replacing him with functioning families who reflect the relationships within the Trinity and the family of God. We will receive and carry the restorative work of the spirit of Elijah to the nations.

Chapter 12: The Head and Not the Tail

It is important that we, God's blood-bought people, realize that it has always been His will for us to be at the top of the mountains in a place of preeminence and blessing. He is not a sadistic God who loves seeing His people struggle and barely survive. Nothing could be further from the truth. He has always sought to motivate us with a promised land of unlimited abundance—body, soul, and spirit. He promised in Deuteronomy 28:13 to make His people "the head and not the tail." For most of Christian history, the world has been the pacesetter and the church has followed its forms by "Christianizing" secular music, art, government, business, and so on. The Elijah Revolution will change that. From the presence of God will flow superior ways of creating arts, conducting business, governing nations, and practicing faith and worship. The world will see the blessing of God on His people, and many will come to Christ from the scent of heaven that the church bears. Like Joshua and Caleb, Elijah revolutionaries will have a different spirit than the Christians who surrender the mountains of culture to the giants who live there. They will not be content to live in a Christian subculture that has little influence on society. They will zealously endeavor to bring entire nations into the kingdom of God.